The Rolls-Royce Companion

'For more than sixty years Rolls-Royce have built motor-cars which have gained a unique position throughout the world with a reputation for unsurpassed quality. The tradition of meticulous attention even to the smallest detail in design and workmanship is followed as closely today as it was in the days of Sir Henry Royce . . .'

The Rolls-Royce Companion

KENNETH ULLYETT

Motorbooks International
Publishers & Wholesalers Inc.

3501 Hennepin Avenue South
Minneapolis, Minnesota 55408, U.S.A.

STANLEY PAUL & CO. LTD
London

AN IMPRINT OF THE   HUTCHINSON GROUP

First published 1969
Reprinted 1973

This book has been printed by offset litho in Great Britain
by Anchor Press and bound by Wm. Brendon,
both of Tiptree, Essex

ISBN 0 09 095350 9

ACKNOWLEDGEMENTS

This book is the sixth in the Companion series. Its first edition is produced in the 60th year of the great Rolls-Royce industrial empire which is responsible for jet engines and equipment for nuclear-powered submarines, for multi-fuel engines and rocket motors. And motor-cars.

What is more important to the reader, this is the first book in the English language to deal solely and comprehensively with the modern Rolls-Royce motor-car. A brief survey is made of past history to put the Company's ramifications and automobile-engineering experience into perspective, and then the story starts with the first post-war Rolls-Royce, the Silver Wraith. It runs through the whole gamut of the present generation of cars, through the Silver Clouds, the Phantoms IV and VI, to the modern Silver Shadow. It deals with engineering developments at Crewe, and discloses research, design and manufacturing stages—all confined to the modern Rolls-Royce.

While I have been given most complete cooperation by Rolls-Royce Ltd., and have been allowed access to material never previously published in book form, this book, like all others in the Companion series, is completely unsponsored by the manufacturers and is compiled with absolute independence from their views. In parts it is critical, and reports impartially and truthfully facts which are not 'good publicity', and which lesser companies than Rolls-Royce might wish to see suppressed. However, these things are not publicity at all, neither good nor bad, but simply facts; things which happened. I believe this is why the Companion series achieves a world-wide sale, since the information given is truthful, factual, useful for the compilers of automobile history, yet acceptable to motoring enthusiasts and others who dream of the day when they, too, may own one of the fine cars described.

In compiling *The Rolls-Royce Companion* I have been given most ready help by many sections of Rolls-Royce Limited at Derby,

Acknowledgements

London and Crewe. In particular I am indebted to officials of the Company including the Rt. Hon. Lord Kindersley, CBE, MC, Sir Denning Pearson, Mr. Whitney W. Straight, CBE, DFC, Dr. F. Llewellyn Smith, CBE, Mr. S. H. Grylls, MA, MIMechE., Mr. A. J. Phillips, Mr. L. Griffiths (chief computing engineer), Mr. D. E. A. Miller-Williams, and to the editors of *The Rolls-Royce Bulletin*, and *Rolls-Royce News*.

As in my *Book of the Silver Ghost* and *Book of the Phantoms*, where it has been possible to include certain technical and historical material previously unpublished in book form, I am indebted to Mr. Kenneth Ball, managing director of Autobooks Limited, for research and the provision of documentary material. I am equally grateful to the Council of the Institution of Mechanical Engineers for permission to republish extracts from papers and discussions dealing with the development of the in-line six and V8 power units. Thanks are also due to the editor of *Autocar*, Elizabeth Benson and Maxwell Boyd (*The Sunday Times*), Tony Brooks, Robert Glenton (*Sunday Express*), Helen Cathcart, *Daily Mail*, London, Mr. Harry Harper, Stirling Moss, the editor *Motor*, The Times Publishing Co. Ltd., Mr. Kenneth Wickham, AMIMechE., and Mr. Tommy Wisdom, for help given in many ways towards the production of this book which, in itself, is a tribute to the one car in the world, maybe the best in the world, which has 'a tradition of meticulous attention to even the smallest detail, both in design and workmanship, followed as closely today as it was in the days of Sir Henry Royce'.

KENNETH ULLYETT

THE ROYAL AUTOMOBILE CLUB
London

CONTENTS

ILLUSTRATIONS

Illustrations

One

ALAS, NO MAGIC

COMMENTING a decade ago in *True's Automobile Yearbook* on 'The one and only Rolls-Royce', Ken W. Purdy opined: 'The Rolls-Royce is not only the best car the world has ever seen, it is very probably the best piston-engined car the world will ever see.

'It is much to be doubted that the predictable future will produce an economy capable of sustaining the kind of workmanship and therefore the money that goes into a Rolls-Royce. One may go further: there is probably no mechanical device in the world as good as a Rolls-Royce. For in no other category of machines does one make possess such obvious overwhelming superiority. No ship is as much superior to other ships as a Rolls is superior to other cars, no airplane, no house or clock or camera, printing press or child's toy. The Rolls-Royce is first. Rolls-Royce is the only firm so sure of its product that it issues a three-year guarantee with each car sold. . . . ' (*Today when a car is sold secondhand within its guarantee period it is the custom of the Company to give the new owner the benefit of the unexpired period of the guarantee.*)

'When a well-cared-for R.-R. turns its first 100,000 miles, it can be considered just nicely broken in. . . . What makes a Rolls so good? There is, alas, no magic. If there were, any car could be as good as a Rolls. . . .'

Ken Purdy then elaborated the theme that the Rolls is good because all connected with the firm, from the chairman of the board to the last foundry sweeper, is determined it shall be so. An absolute refusal to allow anything but the very best obtainable to be put into the car—'from fan-belt to upholsterers' tacks'—characterises everybody connected with the venerable organisation.

Now the inner engineering circles of Derby and Crewe are, after all, only human, and react to being flattered in this way, the policy of Rolls-Royce Limited is to produce 'The Best Car in the World', and while repetition of this very slogan is apt to erupt hot comments from owners of Mercedes-Benz and Maserati, Ferrari and Lamborghini, the Rolls-Royce team wear their 60 glorious years of distinction gracefully and modestly. They are apt to be embarrassed by such effusions such as that in another American periodical I chanced to pick up while researching for this book in the Companion series. The article is headed 'The Nabob's Chariot', and concerns itself almost entirely with an account of the vulgarities which have occasionally been perpetrated in the coachwork of individual R.-R.'s for the gratification of rich eccentrics, Oriental potentates and oil barons. Of the car itself—apart from the excrescences added by owners such as tiger-skin upholstery, elephant-tusk steering wheels, fitted cocktail cabinets with French Empire ormolu fittings, and extra-wide footboards to carry slaves—the highest compliment that the American journalist could muster was that the Rolls-Royce remains: 'Like the Englishmen who make it, ancient, square, strong and dependable.'

Dependable, yes. And as strong as a Rolls-Royce. But ancient and square? Surely this is an inaccurate summing up of the world-wide Rolls-Royce industrial empire which by its 60th year had been honoured three times in succession with Her Majesty the Queen's Award, which employs 85,000 men and women in the United Kingdom, and over 3,000 in overseas countries, which has a gross trading revenue of nearly £180 million (some $400 million) and which, again in its 60th year, won Britain's biggest export order for £150 million worth of jet engines for the Lockheed 1011 300-seater tri-jet airbus. As sales of this aircraft soar in coming years, the value of this contract to Rolls-Royce may run into $1,000 million.

All through this present volume we shall find these links with the world's aircraft and airframe industries, for although Sir Frederick Henry Royce disliked aircraft, and never flew, there would be no Rolls-Royce gas-turbines today but for the Rolls-Royce car: and, of course, the converse. Rolls-Royce piston engines powered the majority of all types of British aircraft in the Second World War and all the fighter aircraft which won the Battle of Britain, their position in the field of military aero engines is still supreme, and on the civil side Rolls-Royce and allied Bristol Siddeley engines have been chosen by 183 airlines. As the finishing touches were being put to proofs of the first edition of this book, a last count by the Company showed that there were 44,500 Rolls-Royce and Bristol Siddeley engines in service throughout the world.

By contrast, the Motor Car Division might at first seem to be very small beer. The Rt. Hon. Lord Kindersley, CBE, MC, chairman of the Company, announced in the summer of 1967 that while a contract having a potential value to the United Kingdom of £35 million was secured in conjunction with the Allison Division of General Motors for the supply of military Spey engines to the United States Government: 'Our motor-car business has a strong order position and the rate of output has improved, but it is faced with special measures to meet the United States' safety regulations.'

In the lifetime of many of us, making automobiles (Rolls-Royce and Bentley) has never been more than 10 per cent of the task of the Company's work, sometimes less. In their entire history, up to the outbreak of the war in 1939, they had manu-factured only 21,800 motor-cars. Even in the resurgent period of the 1950's there was a mere trickle of 20 cars a week coming from Crewe for the world market.

The majority of the world's other noted car makers could not contemplate such restricted, hand-made production—certainly not GM nor Ford, British Leyland nor the busy men in Stuttgart, Wolfsburg and Tokyo. It is all very well to regard the Rolls-Royce as a symbol, but it is one quite beyond the means of far larger car-producing sections of world industry. My friend Macdonald Hastings, in investigating this Best Car in the World legend, reiterated that the monogram 'RR' on the radiator signifies something far greater than a rich man's privilege, and that as to the mystery of what distinguishes Rolls-Royce from all other firms and all other makes of car, there is no secret.

'The Rolls-Royce people themselves,' says Mac, 'will tell you blandly there is no secret. The chassis and engine are based upon established principles and engineering design. There's no alchemy of engineering in a Rolls-Royce car which any motor manufacturer couldn't copy. In fact the firm's chief engineer will assure you that the Americans have the know-how to make a car tomorrow as good as a Rolls-Royce. . . .' By the time you reach the final chapter of this book you will realise why nobody else does make a car so good and in such a way.

In the advertising world where legends are made overnight,

and status-symbols get kicked around, a popular piece of copywriting described a razor, a washing machine, a pram, a cigar or a liqueur as the Rolls-Royce of its kind: and Mr. J. B. M. Adams, the Huntingdonshire purveyor of vintage Rolls-Royce and Bentley motor-cars, told me what he regarded as the ultimate use of The Name as a superlative. It occurred at a meeting of the Royal Dublin Society, when the secretary described the Friesian as 'a type of milk-producing animal known to the man-in-the-street as the Rolls-Royce cow'.

All the same the initial purchaser of a Rolls-Royce car buys more than a cachet, a symbol He buys utter luxury; indeed to most purchasers this is one of the objects of the exercise, and he may care little that he is also buying mechanical excellence and (nowadays, anyway) very advanced design.

Ownership of a Rolls-Royce confers something unobtainable in other ways, and puts the motorist on somewhat the same level as those fortunate few who own an ocean-going yacht or a personal jet airliner. Because of the price tag, the very purchase indicates not only wealth but discernment—and this still applies nowadays when many old, old Royces are painted yellow in foolish imitation of the film, and when pop-singers shock Crewe and the Rolls-Royce zone of Mayfair by having their Silver Clouds sprayed in psychedelic colours and patterns. However, whether this sort of snobbery is inverted or not, it is important to remember that what matters is the tag, not only the price on the tag.

It was around 1951, at a time when the first Silver Dawns were arriving on Fifth Avenue, Sunset Strip and in Dallas, Texas, that a noted motoring correspondent of a New York journal remarked: 'Millionaires, movie-stars, royalty from kings both active and at liberty to fabled Indian maharajahs, have formed the glittering core of R.-R. clientele. But the men of Crewe, England, who make and sell the cars have not erected their present reputation by being out of touch with the times, and the cost of a Rolls-Royce has gone down of late, not up. Inflation may have raised hob with other luxury items, but you can buy a brand-new Rolls-Royce off the peg today for a hair under $10,000 instead of the $15,000–$20,000 they used to cost. That is the price tag on the Silver Dawn model, and it represents a break with R.-R. tradition: the Dawn is the first Rolls ever offered at the factory complete with body. Until the introduction of this model, in 1950, Rolls made chassis only, the bodies being designed and built to customers' specifications by one of the great English coachbuilding firms. The Silver Wraith model, somewhat bigger, is still offered, of course, and sold in the old way: chassis only.'

While costs and prices have risen since those days, there is no doubt that the Best Car in the World is a valid proposition, investment-wise. The British journal *Autocar* went into this thoroughly, and on 4th April, 1968 (at a time when an ill-advised government budget was causing a hardening in used-car values), published a detailed analysis of what a motorist's money would buy. Some 13 cars were picked at random from dealers' advertisements, the cars checked thoroughly and the financial aspects such as depreciation (in some cases appreciation), running costs and so forth examined. 'Finally,' they reported, 'we included a Rolls in the year's series—a 1962 Rolls-Royce Silver Cloud III, on the market at £3,450. It was faultless in every way except for a slight deterioration of the brakes, and all but one of the acceleration figures timed from rest to 100 mph were within a second of the original Road Test figures measured in 1960. After the test of this fine car, we added a new figure to the Used Car Test data—annual depreciation, expressed as a percentage of the purchase cost. It reveals that the rate of loss with the Rolls was only 9 per cent of the original investment per year. . . .'

A far-seeing Rolls-Royce owner will also look far beyond that 9 per cent. This has been emphasised in print from fashion-plates to cartoon strips, and an amusing instance of the latter is the 'J.J.' Business Tycoon character portrayed by Roy Dewar in the *Sunday Express*. In half a dozen cartoon balloons, J.J. forcefully lectures his co-directors: 'I will not have expenditure on modernisation thwarted. . . . People are all too ready to accuse us of dragging our feet . . . by clinging to the past. . . . How can I hope to convince the world at large that we are a thrusting, go-ahead, dynamic, forward-looking enterprise . . . *in a last year's Rolls?*'

Of course there are those who object, or raise difficulties. There was the occasion, for instance, when that noted pioneer of the art of strip-tease, Gipsy Rose Lee, was touring Yugoslavia in her Rolls-Royce, with her 14-year-old son. They were astounded when a motor-cyclist with a pillion passenger came suddenly out of a side lane and ran into the back of their car, luckily without serious damage. Gipsy's boy got out to see if the couple on the motor-cycle were injured, only to find to his amazement that they left their machine in the road and skeltered out of sight. The London *Daily Mail*, reporting this incident, said that Gipsy felt the only thing possible in this extraordinary circumstance was to drive on to the next town and report it to the police. But when she pressed for an explanation the police told her: 'Madame, it is well known there are only two Rolls-Royces in the whole of Yugoslavia—and both belong to Marshal Tito.'

From such true incidents do Rolls-Royce legends grow. By contrast there is the apocryphal story of the Rolls-Royce owner who unfortunately had the splines of a crankshaft shear during some hard driving on a Continental journey, so wired the Works and had a new shaft sent out air freight. On returning from holiday he was somewhat surprised to find that Rolls-Royce Ltd. had not yet sent an invoice, and when he telephoned Crewe they told him they had no record of any such incident.

'But you must know about it,' insisted the customer. 'You flew one out to me. I was touring abroad, and I had a crankshaft go.'

'Sir,' came the reply, 'Rolls-Royce crankshafts do not go.'

As I say, the story is apocryphal. In real life, invoices for R.-R. spares are dispatched just as promptly as the spares themselves. Although the Company spends an average of £6,800,000 a year on research and development, it is not a benevolent society. There is no more than the usual trading profit out of the United Kingdom price of a shade over £6,000 for a standard Silver Shadow, and no doubt if it were not for the R.-R. aero-engine division there would be no cars being manufactured at all at Crewe: well, not as cheaply as £6,000 each. Nevertheless, for the ordinary man it *is* a great deal of money to pay for a car, and as was said by Mr. Ian S. Hallows, editor of *The 20-Ghost Club Record*, in his journal produced for this erudite and elect group of owners of vintage Royces: 'Your editor noticed that the first time he went in a Silver Shadow the loudest sound that could be heard was the beating of his bank-manager's heart.'

Just before Dr. F. Llewellyn Smith, CBE, relinquished his position as managing director of the Motor Car Division for another senior directorate position, I had the opportunity of discussing in detail these very matters of the Legend, and of the Cost. On the former he said modestly: 'Well I think you may put it this way—we are the trustees of a national inheritance.' And as to the cost, we talked in general terms about one of the earliest Silver Ghosts which was sold at a Sotheby's auction for £9,800 to James Leake, owner of three television stations in Oklahoma and also of seven other Rolls-Royces. This shows an enormous appreciation in the value of a 1911 car, and Dr. Llewellyn Smith said: 'Taking these figures, I have worked out that in 1983 a current Silver Shadow could be worth £38,000.'

Of course increasing prices and consequent market inflation have been going on all the time, and who can check this? In 1904 the price of the very first Rolls-Royce car marketed—a two-cylinder 10 hp of 1·8 litres' capacity, with a tonneau body —was £395. The Legalimit (the first V-8 by Rolls-Royce) carried a price tag of £1,140 in 1906, whereas in January, 1914, the price of the Silver Ghost chassis was still held at £985, $8,000 in the United States, and it is this type of early Ghost which now commands fantastic auction values at least ten times greater than when new. However, the effects of rising costs were noticeable even half a century ago, and when the first Silver Ghost catalogue appeared immediately after the First World War (the Ghost was the only model then being produced), the listed price of the vaunted London–Edinburgh open four-seater was £1,154 15s.

Some Rolls-Royce legends are so patently untrue that, like the story of the crankshafts, they cause the men of Crewe to wince slightly each time the tale boomerangs. When Press and television reporters interview top technical executives of the Motor Car Division there is a natural demand for bigger and better stories. Dr. Llewellyn Smith, when head of the Division, and Mr. S. H. Grylls, MA, as chief engineer, were frequently having to face this sort of Press barrage, and the time came when a girl interviewer of a top New York journal was granted a session because she wanted to apotheosise any scrap of any new legend which Mr. Grylls could recall about The Best Car in the World.

'Yes,' he said after reflection, 'there does in fact come to my mind a little incident going right back to the days when Sir Henry Royce was trying out an experimental chassis in the South of France. He was angry when on one occasion the horn button stuck. In those days, of course, the whole current for the Klaxon went through the switch, so Sir Henry immediately issued instructions to the Works that henceforth all horn buttons must have gold contacts.

'Of course, this overcame the trouble, but perhaps through some little oversight in the drawing office we went on turning out cars with gold horn contacts even when later techniques came in and all such electrical accessories were relay-operated.'

It was a true and an amusing story, but Crewe may not have been amused when the story appeared in the United States, after maltreatment by the re-write subs. '*Rolls-Royce*,' the column was headed, '*The Car with the Solid Gold Horn Button.*'

True anecdotes of Rolls-Royce motor-cars, and of the men who designed and built them, are told in many books including the Foulis publications *The Magic of a Name* by Harold Nockolds and *A History of Rolls-Royce Motorcars* (Vol. 1) by C. W. Morton which, like my own volumes *The Book of the Silver Ghost* and *The Book of the Phantoms*, deal chiefly with the vintage period. This present book, however, deals with post-war models from 1947 on. Although the central image of Rolls-Royce itself has not changed since the era of the Hon. Charles Rolls and Sir Henry Royce, neither of them could have foreseen the changes to come in the design philosophy, the ever-increasing scope of the Rolls-Royce industrial empire, and of course in the cars themselves.

Putting the post-war models in chronological order, the dictum of the 20-Ghost Club must be accepted that the 'collector's' period begins with the handful of Manchester-built cars of 1904–6, and ends with the last Derby-built cars of 1939.

The first post-war model is therefore the Silver Wraith, which appeared in 1947. However, as we shall see in a later chapter detailing this model, many years of development went by before 1947, and meanwhile the Derby-built Wraith (production of which was commenced in 1936) was in full spate of production until 1939. Although the Company was concerned in preparation for military production from about 1936, manufacture of the Wraith was not ended immediately on the advent of war. In fact a few Wraiths were not delivered until 1940, so in a sense the original Wraith crosses this historic gap of years. While there are no post-war Wraiths there are some which one might term 'inter-war.'

Its successor the Silver Wraith has so far been the third most popular model of the post-war production schedule, and about

1,800 were built during the 13-year period 1947-59. There were three essential changes following the 1947 prototype, in 1951, 1955 and 1957. An early-series Silver Wraith has collectors' value nowadays, as well as being in every sense a modern-specification motor-car.

First in the Silver Wraith series is the 4,257-cc version ($3\frac{1}{2}$-in. bore, $4\frac{1}{2}$-in. stroke) with manual gearbox. This was available in short wheelbase (127-in.) and long (133-in.) versions, and the price of the chassis was £1,800. In 1951 the engine capacity was increased to 4,566 cc by boring out to $3\frac{5}{8}$ in., and automatic transmission was introduced in 1952. The capacity was again increased in 1955, this time to 4,887 cc, by a $3\frac{3}{4}$-in. bore. During 1957-9 the last cars in the Silver Wraith series had the compression ratio increased from 6·75 to 8·0:1.

Immediate success of this first post-war Rolls-Royce prompted the introduction of a slightly different design, the first of which were left-hand drive, for export, although today some of the best examples are right-hand drive models which stayed in the United Kingdom. This series is the Silver Dawn, the design essentials and production programme of which overlap those of the Silver Wraith. While usually regarded as a much smaller car than the Silver Wraith, the Silver Dawn has a wheelbase of 120 in., compared with the 127 in. of the first-series Silver Wraiths. With any Rolls-Royce, smallness is really in the eye of the beholder, and the standard-steel coachwork on the Dawn—primarily, as Ken Purdy said, 'offered at the factory complete with body'—was overall shorter than most of the coachwork fitted to the Silver Wraiths in the early 1950's. The Silver Dawn was in production from 1949 to 1955. At first it had the 4,257-cc engine, and the larger 4,566-cc power unit from 1951. By 1952 there was automatic transmission with an overriding control on the steering-column. As export versions of the Silver Wraith had the manual box with steering-column shift (rare, for Rolls-Royce Ltd.), admirers of these older models have to peer closely into the driving compartment to see if it is a GM-type automatic box with a column lever, or a Rolls-Royce manual box with a similar column-mounted shift. It is generally thought that because it was designed with overseas users in mind, and as the market widened so considerably after the introduction of the Silver Cloud in 1955, the Silver Dawn was not high in Crewe's production totals. However, it appears 760 Silver Dawns were built, which, of course, is considerably more than the pre-war Wraith (490), and 50 more than the total production of the legendary V-12 Phantom III, of which only 710 came on the market.

In a sense all these immediate post-war cars were 'little' Rolls-Royces, the largest engine capacity being 4,887 cc, and they were growing-up versions of that first true little Rolls-Royce, the Twenty, of 1922–9. Of course, in those earlier days there was always a 'bigger' Rolls-Royce as well, the Phantom I (the New Phantom), the Phantoms II and III, and it was only the recession after the Second World War which induced the Company to concentrate on these modern derivations of the 'Twenty' formula that in turn had been 20, 20/25, 25/30 and Wraith.

In time for 1950, however, changing world conditions once more seemed to indicate the need for a larger companion to the Silver Wraith and Silver Dawn, and production was started of the first and only straight-eight Rolls-Royce ever to go into series manufacture at the Works. This is the Phantom IV, of which legend has it that 'all the customers were Royal,' and which did indeed find favour with H.M. Queen Elizabeth and Princess Margaret for State use. (In private, the Queen was frequently seen in a Rover, an Alvis or a blue Mini, while Princess Margaret was sometimes a Mini-Cooper passenger.) The Phantom IV's technical innovations are dealt with in a later chapter, but the series was in production only from 1950 to 1956, and 18 were built.

No price has ever been placed on the Phantom IV, since no stripped chassis were delivered to private owners. All purchasers, whether of Royal stock or of ordinary red blood like the rest of us, had special coachwork fitted to order. As an indication of values, however, the Silver Dawn chassis was being made available to coachbuilders at about £2,500 during this Phantom IV period, and it is improbable the Phantom IV could have been offered at under two and a half times the cost of a Silver Dawn. This would be the equivalent of £12,000 15 years later when the first Silver Shadows went into production.

While the Silver Wraith and Silver Dawn were commanding a world market, the Company made a considerable step forward in modern design by the introduction in 1955 of the Silver Cloud, now better known as the 'Cloud I'. This '£5,858 worth of mechanical perfection', as one motoring columnist dubbed it, was a companion to the Rolls-Bentley S.1. They shared the same standard steel saloon body. Only the radiator shells and the motifs on hub-caps and bumpers (fenders) differed. Transmission is automatic, without manual as an option, and while there was a convertible body available in very limited production on the short-wheelbase 123-in. version, a range of special coachwork was to be had on the 4-in. longer model. In either case the chassis was marketed at £3,385. For three years the Cloud remained unmodified, one of the most popular of post-war Rolls-Royce cars, but in 1958 to make use of higher-octane fuels and to ensure, perhaps, that no Rolls-Royce owner was distraught too frequently at being overtaken, the compression ratio of the 4,887 cc engine was increased from 6·6 to 8:1.

During these commercially busy years Crewe did not rest on its laurels, and as we shall see in a later section concerned with the sequence of Rolls-Royce engine design, there was increasing marketing pressure to have V-8 power units with the type of automatic transmission used. Thus, in 1958, came the Silver Cloud II, which proved to be an even more important design turning point than many of us supposed at its introduction.

For one thing, with its big 6,230 cc engine, it was the first time since the era of the old Silver Ghost that the Company were marketing a 'big' car only. The body-shell remained virtually unchanged, but with the V-8 engine this 4,588-lb car has a very impressive performance. Some 2,700 Cloud II's were built, until in 1962 the Silver Cloud III was introduced. Bentley models S.2 and S.3 are comparable.

In our present complex social situation world sales of any car depend not only upon price, performance, specification and prestige, but also on such factors as potential tax deductibility and whether 'the firm's going to foot the bill'. At various periods people gullible enough to credit such rumours believed that In- come Tax inspectors and professional accountants were—equally —gullible enough to regard a Bentley as a 'firm's car', and there- fore eligible for a better rate of tax allowances than a Rolls-Royce. This may have had a germ of truth in it back in the years when there was an appreciable price differential, but whatever the reason may be, it is known that 4,946 of the first Crewe-built Mark VI Bentleys were sold, compared with only 1,800 of the somewhat similar Silver Wraith. Moving on a few years, the

2,360 sales of the Silver Cloud I compare with 3,009 of the almost identical Bentley S.1.

Stories are told of the lady who sent her chauffeur out to buy one of these cars, and lifted her monocle in angry surprise when he appeared at the drive gates in a Bentley instead of a Cloud.

'I told you to get the one with the *square* radiator,' she said, according to the strip-cartoon artist who first put this story into the ranks of the Rolls-Royce legends.

There were S.1, 2 and 3 owners who scorned the Rolls-Royce version as being 'too ostentatious' or 'a damned sight too much when you go shopping and the little tradesmen charge you Rolls-Royce prices', or simply 'unpopular with my accountant, old man'. All of this says much for the esoteric symbolism of those magic initials 'RR', since in most respects except The Name these Bentley and Rolls-Royce models are identical: and Bentley is a Top Name anyway.

However, there are State occasions when even a Silver Cloud may not be luxurious enough, and for such purposes the Company introduced the Phantom V in 1959. It is a long-wheelbase car, 114 in., with a similar power unit and transmission to that used in the Cloud II and Cloud III, but the extra few inches of chassis length allow special coachwork to be mounted. The Royal stable took delivery of one of the first Phantom V's to come off the line, and a number of cars used by similar Very Important People and Heads of State have been modified to the later version known as the Phantom V Mark II. At length, in October 1968, the Phantom VI was produced, incorporating engine changes also introduced for the Silver Shadow.

It goes without saying that some coachwork fitted on the Phantom V is unique, and in future years will command high prices from collectors; however, in their day there are a good many cars more expensive than this Royal model, the chassis of which bore a basic price tag in 1959 of £3,130 plus tax.

Following repeated rumours that the Company was entering the mini-car market, or introducing a front-drive or a rear-engine model, in 1965 the revolutionary monocoque Silver Shadow appeared, low-cut, silent, with all-electric accessories, extremely speedy, the complete answer to the critic who had summed up the Royce image as 'ancient, square'.

These, then, are the cars which form the subject of this book.

What of the Company which builds them, and of which, let's face it, the Motor Car Division is now a pretty small digit? One cannot ignore the ramjets and turbofans, hovercraft engines and Polaris-submarine plant when buying Rolls-Royce cars, nor even when writing about them; for much of the advanced research, current technology and range of manufacturing skills is woven into every inch of the Rolls-Royce fabric. The question of 'What *is* Rolls-Royce?' frequently arises, also, among Rolls-Royce owners and others who know the group is a blue-chip investment, yet are continually being pleasantly surprised at its ramifications.

At the time of completing the first (1969–70) edition of this book, the question 'Who *are* Rolls-Royce?' could best be answered by saying that from Nightingale Road, Derby (the original HQ of the Company opened by the first Lord Montagu of Beaulieu in July, 1908), the fortunes of this great network, with a gross trading revenue of over £171 million, are controlled by a board headed by the Rt. Hon. Lord Kindersley, CBE, MC (chairman), Sir Denning Pearson (deputy chairman and chief executive), Whitney W. Straight, CBE, MC, DFC (deputy chairman), and Sir W. Reginald Verdon-Smith (vice chairman). The directorate had been changed in 1966, consequent upon the merger with The Bristol Aeroplane Co. Ltd. and Bristol Siddeley Engines Ltd. Sir Reginald Verdon-Smith was formerly chairman of Bristol's, and Mr. W. Masterton deputy chairman. Mr. Hugh Conway, CBE, was managing director of Bristol Siddeley Engines. They had long association in the aviation field with Rolls-Royce Ltd. and by joining the R.-R. board added experience and strength to the main team. Although relinquishing his position as managing director of the Motor Car Division in 1968, Dr. F. Llewellyn Smith, CBE, joined the main board and continued to be the Rolls-Royce director responsible for the Motor Car and Oil Engine divisions; he is also chairman of their divisional boards.

Another important change in the Rolls-Royce board came in July, 1967. Mr. W. T. Gill had joined the Company in 1939 and was appointed financial director in 1946. In the following years he accepted further heavy responsibilities and among his other duties served a second term of office as President of the Society of British Aerospace Companies. He retired in October from an executive post. Mr. H. W. Trevan-Hawke was therefore appointed to the R.-R. board as financial controller in mid-1967 and Mr. Gill continued as an executive director with particular responsibility for forward financial planning.

How rich is Rolls-Royce? With usually around half a million pounds sterling at the bank, and about £108 million stock, in plain English the Rolls-Royce group runs as a £151 million concern, of which the goodwill, patents and trademarks alone account for £25 million.

Extremists in political thinking have knocked this blue-chip bastion by calling it Capitalist Stuff, but this criticism (if such it can be called) is not valid when you come to discover who the capitalists are. They are you and I. The institutions and the unit trusts and the many thousands of small savers are all safely 'in Rolls'. The secured debenture stock comes out at £37 million, and after the authorised Ordinary stock of £45½ million (widely held by small investors) there are £2½ million of Workers' (1955) stock units of 10s. each; so when one talks of capitalists having their money in Rolls-Royce, some of these are the Little Capitalists who work at the presses, assembly lines and in the test-cells.

There is no secrecy about the directorate, nor the way in which Rolls-Royce works. In addition to those directors named, the changes in 1968 brought on the Motor Car Division board Mr. G. Fawn as successor to Dr. Llewellyn Smith (previously a deputy managing director), Mr. R. E. Garner (director and materials manager), Mr. I. D. Nelson (director of personnel and administration), Mr. T. Neville (financial controller) and Mr. L. S. Poulton (director and production manager). These are among the men who guide the destinies of Rolls-Royce motor-cars, and through Dr. Llewellyn Smith they are represented on the board of the main company.

Rolls-Royce is democratic to a degree never visualised in the early days of Rolls and Royce and Claude Johnson. Nowadays the interests of all the directors and their family interests do not in the aggregate, in respect of either share capital or voting control, exceed 5 per cent of the company, or of any one subsidiary. Apart from the Workers' (1955) stock (of which about £1,800,000 is held by R.-R. employees in service, the rest by those retired), well over half a million pounds worth of Ordinary stock is also held by present and retired workers, which shows that the men and women who build Rolls-Royce know it is a good investment.

Above Sir Henry Royce ('R') (*right*) at Le Canadel, outside his villa La Mimosa, the building of which was started in 1912, and from where, owing to ill-health, he directed the engineering fortunes of Rolls-Royce Ltd for many years, and personally tried out new models on the highways of the South of France

Below Silver Shadow four-door saloon, with V-8 6,230 cc engine, hydraulically-operated height-control system, electric control of automatic transmission, and a triplicated power braking system. Independent rear suspension, monocoque steel body and other design-features emphasise the 40-year gap between the two Rolls-Royce cars shown on this page

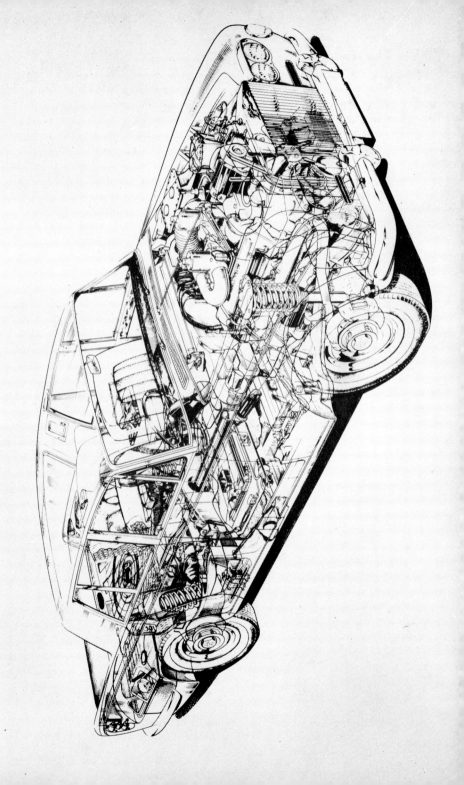

Above Cut-away perspective diagram of the Silver Shadow, showing closed box section frame of welded steel construction, independent front and rear suspension (with electrical control of hydraulic rear dampers), and divided-type propeller shaft having a ball and trunnion universal joint at front, and needle-roller joint at centre and rear

Below Cut-away perspective drawing of the Rolls-Royce V-8 power unit, of the type first introduced at the end of 1958 for the Silver Cloud II, and subsequently developed for the Cloud III (1962), the Phantom V (1959), the Silver Shadow (from 1965), and the Phantom VI (from 1968)

Above Rolls-Royce automatic gearbox of the type first introduced in 1953 for the Silver Dawn, subsequently developed for the Clouds, Phantom V and Silver Shadow. This cut-away model on an exhibition stand shows the gear-selector mechanism and hydraulic valves
Below Silver Cloud III chassis of 1964, the last of this series before the introduction of the monocoque-construction Silver Shadow. Grand Prix driver Tony Brooks tested a Silver Cloud III standard saloon, weighing some 2 tons, at Goodwood. He lapped in well under two minutes, consistently touching 103 mph

Other than employees, over £21 million of Ordinary stock is held by individuals, and slightly more than this total by the banks, the insurance and investment companies, the educational and religious bodies, the charitable institutions and pension funds who know that Rolls-Royce is as safe as—well, as safe as Rolls-Royce.

Much of the strength of the Motor Car Division now comes as we have seen from the fact that the Company develops, researches-into and builds so many other things than motor-cars. It is easy to say that the aviation activities account for 86 per cent of the Company's activities, because such a brief statement is apt to imply that the remaining 14 per cent (which includes the cars) is of lesser importance. It is not.

R.-R. aero-engine facilities at Sinfin, Derby, cover a wide area and include a large altitude plant for testing engines under simulated flight conditions, at speeds up to Mach 2·4 and heights to over 70,000 ft. The computer hall at Derby contains solid-state devices by which Rolls-Royce can now apply computer techniques on a very wide scale, in a sphere never dreamed of by Rolls nor by Royce. And both these individualists might be startled at the current joint aero-engine international programmes: Rolls-Royce and Bristol Siddeley are working with companies in France, Germany and the United States on joint development of at least six turbine engines, the Olympus 593, Adour, M 45, RB 193, Spey TF 41, and the advanced lift jet. Moreover, licences for the manufacture of Rolls-Royce engines are held by companies in Australia, Belgium, India, Italy, Sweden, Switzerland and Yugoslavia.

In 1967 the Company formed a new division to handle all industrial and marine gas turbine business, with headquarters at Ansty, near Coventry. More than 450 Olympus, Avon, Proteus, Tyne and Gnome industrial and marine turbines are in service or on order throughout the world, totalling £15 million in the first year. The K-range multi-fuel engines, B-range petrol engines for crash-trucks, military vehicles and fire appliances (there are even Jeeps with Rolls-Royce engines), the nuclear plant for submarines, built by Rolls-Royce & Associates Ltd., the Rolls-Royce RZ.2 rocket motors at Woomera ('delivering 150,000 lb. thrust at lift-off') . . . All these, and more, seem to dwarf our basic interest, the Rolls-Royce motor-car. Yet, you see, it is the Rolls-Royce motor-car which—following the dynamos and incandescent lamps of Royce Ltd, in Manchester, in the '80's—began the whole story.

That comment 'Like the Englishmen who make it, ancient, square', and so on, is no longer true in technical fact. The radiator on the present cars is very low, yet appears to retain its geometric form evoking the pediment and columns of the Parthenon. But square? No. Not any more. As Mr. Grylls remarked to Gordon Wilkins when he admired the radiator shell of the Silver Shadow: 'If you look very closely you will observe that it is slightly curved in plan view as a concession to the age in which we live.'

Two

THE GOOD OLD DAYS?

'EVERY car is individually built and tested with the utmost care by skilled craftsmen', Rolls-Royce Ltd say in their current sales literature. 'The tradition of meticulous attention to even the smallest detail, both in design and workmanship, of Rolls-Royce and Bentley motor-cars is followed as closely today as it was in the days of Sir Henry Royce.'

So the present-day Rolls-Royce owner may well wonder what the days of Sir Henry Royce were really like, and whether, if the legend did begin then, the link has in reality been maintained. Henry Ford is long since dead, and although he left his mark on Detroit his philosophies simply do not show themselves in the present generation of cars, any more than one can see the influence of Lord Austin or of Viscount Nuffield in the current products of the vast British Leyland group; so it is not idle curiosity to ask if in truth there is anything of Rolls or of Royce in the modern Rolls-Royce apart from the initials on the radiator. (The present Silver Shadow does not even have 'RR' on the horn button.) To answer this question, let us turn back for a brief while to the old days, and see for ourselves.

So much has been written about the Hon. Charles Stewart Rolls and Sir Frederick Henry Royce, the almost casual meeting of these two great Englishmen, and the combination of triumph and tragedy that led to everlasting fame. There is a rather dull park in Derby known locally as the Arboretum, in which stands a statue of Royce. 'Born 1863 at Alwalton, near Peterborough', the inscription reads. 'Owing to misfortunes in childhood he was almost entirely self-educated. His work included the design and production of the Rolls-Royce motor-cars of world-wide reputation which were used for most important work in the Great War, and also the design of the Rolls-Royce aero engines. . . . Aeroplanes with these engines made the first direct flight across the Atlantic in 16 hours, and the first flight from England to Australia.'

Royce was such a great man and his work so profoundly affected British engineering and even world thinking, that a wider view of him can be taken. Not only did he influence the science of locomotion on land and in the air, but his basic methods and superlative standards raised the very thought on this subject to an art. He never claimed to be a pioneer, but constantly persevered towards perfection by incessant improvement: and I suppose it is obvious this applies to the present generation of Rolls-Royce cars.

The great Company of Rolls-Royce Limited was brought into being by this self-taught GNR locomotive apprentice Henry Royce, by the Hon. Charley Rolls, son of Baron Llangattock and a pioneer motorist, balloonist and aviator, and by Claude Goodman Johnson (now known as 'the hyphen between Rolls and Royce'), who earned a great reputation in the dawn of motoring as founder-secretary of the Automobile Club which in time became the RAC. Rolls, as most schoolboys know, was killed when his Wright biplane stalled after the collapse of a rear elevator during the Bournemouth Air Meeting of 12th July, 1910. Soon afterwards Royce became seriously ill, largely as the result of early years of overwork and malnutrition, and Claude Johnson exiled him to the South of France years before the New Phantom (successor to the Silver Ghost) was on his drawing-board. Johnson himself died in April, 1926, barely a year after the New Phantom was to be seen. Other great men have carried on their traditions, as we shall see.

With the sort of engineering snobbery which affects all of us who love cars, it is fashionable to speak of a 'Royce', and not a Rolls-Royce, because Royce was the designer, the engineer, the builder. Fortunately, Claude Johnson was that unique combination of an organiser and a visionary. And Rolls? A Rolls-Royce historian summed him up as 'probably the finest driver and most imaginative motoring authority of his day'. Harry Harper, a contemporary, says: 'Those of us who knew him will never forget Charley Rolls. He was a pioneer in every sense of the word—a living embodiment of a new era. In his all-too-short life he wrote his name on history in a way that was imimperishable.'

Of course these men were not saints, any more or less than others. The truth is vivid and often cruel.

Frederick Henry Royce, known by his initial 'R' in the

great Company he helped to found, even after his knighthood, was simply 'Fred' to everyone in his boyhood apprentice years at the Great Northern Railway locomotive works. Son of a Peterborough miller, his father died when Royce was nine, leaving the family penniless. He had only one year of schooling, sold newspapers at W. H. Smith's news-stand at Clapham Junction and Bishopsgate stations, became a telegraph boy at a Mayfair post office. His mother worked as a housekeeper, and an aunt promised to raise a £20-a-year premium (a great deal of money in the 1880's) to send Fred to the GNR. Unfortunately this good lady's circumstances changed within three years and the boy had to quit his training and find another job. This was Victorian England. A Leeds firm of tool-makers supplying the Italian Arsenal paid him 11s. for a 54-hour week often working from 6 am until 10 pm. Then back to London to work with a pioneer electric-power company, and eventually to Liverpool, where Royce was installing street electric lighting before he was 20 years of age.

With a friend Ernest Claremont he decided to set up on his own as an electrical engineer. He had saved £20. Claremont added £50. With this they took a small workshop in Cooke Street, Manchester, producing electric fittings, bells and dynamos. Within 10 years the little concern of F. H. Royce & Co. became a £30,000 public company. The story of how Royce became a pioneer automobilist, bought a French-built Decauville, then decided to build a better vehicle in his own private workshop, is now familiar history.

Harry Harper, to whom I have already referred, was the first air correspondent in Britain, perhaps in the world; he was picked by Lord Northcliffe because he had already done some ballooning. 'Sometimes,' recalled Harper, 'it hardly seems possible in these bleak days to recapture even in memory those Edwardian times when one could live life to the full, without a care or worry to mar the scene. I remember driving down with Rolls to Ranelagh for one of our Aero Club balloon events: on the gay lawns, under a warm summer sun, fashionable London had assembled to see a number of big yellow balloons go sailing up into the sky.

'That day Rolls was acting as "hare" in a hare-and-hounds balloon contest. I remember watching him go up alone in a small balloon, with a basket just big enough for one occupant, and in the face of an approaching storm. . . . For Rolls as a driver of motor-cars I never lost my admiration. As soon as he settled himself at the wheel he appeared to become just part of the car he was handling. Man and machine seemed one.'

It is incorrect, however to classify Rolls simply as one of the fearless motoring pioneers. He was no daredevil. His technical knowledge was considerable. He left Cambridge with a degree in Mechanics and Applied Science. And apart from flirting with death in a yellow balloon, he had quite extensive motor-business interests and spent a good deal of time in car racing and reliability trials. As early as 1900, Charley Rolls in a 12-hp much-photographed Panhard won the 1,000 Miles Reliability Trial promoted by Northcliffe. Three years later he established a world land-speed record at Phoenix Park, Dublin, at the wheel of an 80-hp. Mors.

From his London business of C. S. Rolls & Co., Charley Rolls sold the cars he drove and raced, including Panhard, Mors, Whitlock-Aster, the New Orleans (a British edition of the Belgian Vivinus, built at Orleans, Twickenham), as well as the Gardner-Serpollet steam-car. His partner in this thriving business was Claude Johnson, whose name stood high with pioneer motorists (and potential customers) because of his work in founding the Automobile Club, in Whitehall Court. C. S. Rolls & Co. had a showroom in Brook Street, Mayfair, and a repair shop in Lillie Hall, Fulham. From this workshop they were official repairers to the War Office and (after King Edward VII so blessed it) the Royal Automobile Club.

While Claude Johnson kept Rolls and Royce together— sometimes in itself a difficult task—and was Royce's strong right arm after the untimely aircrash at Bournemouth, he did not actually bring Rolls and Royce together. This honour goes to Henry Edmunds, a shareholder in one of Claremont's other companies and who as a committee member of the Royal Automobile Club naturally knew Charley Rolls. Edmunds, through a fortunate chance, was loaned one of the experimental 10-hp cars which Royce built in Manchester (only three sets of castings were budgeted for, and Edmunds' car was the second to be constructed), and in the spring of 1904 he wrote that now-classic letter: 'My dear Rolls: I have pleasure in enclosing you the photographs and specifications of the Royce car, which I think you will agree with me looks very promising. . . . Knowing, as I do, the skill of Mr. Royce as a practical mechanical engineer, I feel sure one is very safe in taking up any work his firm may produce.'

Royce and Rolls, at first both too busy to meet, at length agreed to Henry Edmunds acting as umpire at their discussions. Years afterwards Edmunds revealed: 'I well remember the conversation I had in the dining-car of the train with Mr. Rolls, who said it was his ambition to have a motor-car connected with his name so that in the future it might be a household word, just as much as Broadwood or Steinway in connection with pianos, or Chubb in connection with safes. . . . I remember we went to the Great Central Hotel at Manchester and lunched together. I think both men took to each other at first sight.'

Rolls' wish came true. In the early years of the Silver Ghost a catalogue copywriter put it this way: 'The man who goes to Poole's for his clothes, Purdy for his guns and Hardy for his rods, goes to Rolls-Royce for his car.'

All the top men of the R.-R. team were known by initials or abbreviations of their names. Thus, Royce, of course, R, Rolls CSR, and Claude Johnson CJ. Others included Hs (Ernest Walter Hives, later to become first Baron Hives), Rg (engine designer A. J. Rowledge), Ep (Eric Platford), W (Arthur Wormald, a tool-maker who joined R from Westinghouse, and later became works manager and a director of Rolls-Royce Ltd), and Ev (H. I. F. Evernden, with the Company for 45 years, and for many years chief project engineer of the Motor Car Division). Charles Rolls was the first managing director, just as Dr. Llewellyn Smith became the first managing director of the Motor Car Division. However, while Llewellyn Smith joined the Derby group two months after the death of Sir Henry Royce, so cannot claim the honour of being a personal link with the present, this honour does go to Mr. S. H. Grylls, MA., MIMechE, MSIA, MSAE, appointed chief engineer of the Motor Car Division in 1951. He came into Rolls-Royce via Rugby, and Trinity College, Cambridge.

Most powerful link between the old world and the new at Rolls-Royce was Hs, who died on 24th April, 1965, at the age of 79, after a lifetime with the Company of which he became chairman. He joined as a test driver in 1908, and his qualities carried him first to the position of head of the Experimental Department, then to works manager, and director. It was largely because of

Hs's inspiration and leadership that Rolls-Royce was able to make a contribution to the war effort that was second to none. I knew him best during those years, and until his retirement in 1957, by which time he had laid the foundation of the plan on which the present cars (and indeed many other aspects of Rolls-Royce world-wide industry) are based.

Like R himself (of whom even an official Rolls-Royce-approved report stated: 'Royce, a grim, ascetic-looking bearded North Countryman, a fanatic . . . he dedicated his life, with the single-track purpose of a barefooted pilgrim, to making beautiful machines. "You can't be an engineer," he once said, "and go to church." ') he was not an easy man to work for. It was against his principles that sentiment should influence business decisions, and he could be tough, even ruthless, when necessary. He never seemed remote from the men and women who worked for him, and maybe that was because he started life with few advantages. In 1898 he began as an apprentice with a Reading engineering concern, but in Hs's eyes it had one advantage. The firm owned a horseless carriage, and, as Hs told me, 'I'd made up my mind I was going to get mixed up with those contraptions.'

On completion of his apprenticeship, he joined C. S. Rolls & Co. as an improver-fitter, working at the Lillie Road workshop in the company of Claude Johnson and Rolls himself, neither of whom were afraid of grease. For reasons I've never been able to recall, Hs did not go straight to Derby when the association with Royce was formed, but went instead to the 'enemy', Napiers. However, in 1908, he moved to Rolls-Royce and after a period as a test-driver worked for Ep (Platford) in the Experimental Department. Hs was then 22.

By 1912, Hs was acknowledged to be one of the most capable men in the department, and a skilled driver. Royce chose him for the now-classic trial of the Silver Ghost to beat the performance of a Napier driven in top gear from London to Edinburgh, concluding with a speed test at Brooklands. His Ghost averaged over 24 miles to the gallon on the run, and lapped Brooklands at 78·26 mph. Later he took a stripped Ghost chassis over the flying-start half-mile at Brooklands at 101·8 mph, and in 1912 handled one of the three works Ghosts which, plus a private entry, made history in the Austrian Alpine Trial.

Hs's work in the Experimental Department (of which he was

manager for 20 years) kept him in close touch with Royce, and no doubt there were many disputes between the two since it was Hs's job to prove design weaknesses in car and aero-engine projects. But there was a lurking sense of humour in Hs's make-up which helped to keep the most difficult situation in perspective, and enabled him to drive himself and others beyond the limit when necessary. Personal anecdote gets tedious. The facts are that he ended the First World War in charge of the Experimental Department, leading his team to manufacture in record time the R engines for Britain's Schneider Trophy seaplanes of 1929 and 1931. For the latter they completed in nine months what *Flight* has described as 'five years of normal development work'.

Such was the man who, in the autumn of 1936 (the start of the successful Phantom III period on the R.-R. car-production side, and when the Wraith was being planned), was appointed general works manager, becoming a director the following spring. The Merlin engine was taking its place in the re-equipment of the Royal Air Force, and many saw in the Phantom III a scaled down car-engine version of the Merlin.

With the coming fears of another world war, the Air Ministry stepped up its demands for Merlins, and by 1938 it was obvious that Derby alone could not handle the engine programme. So Hs settled on Crewe as the right place for the new factory. This factory where the cars are now built was constructed by the Air Ministry, leased to Rolls-Royce and run as part of the Company's organisation. Development of Crewe has been a typical Hs project. Its first machined parts were available four and a half months after the factory went up. Its first engine was on the test bed on 20th May, 1939, 11 months after the first sod was cut.

The story of the Rolls-Royce major contribution to the war effort has been told many times, but there is one story, little known, which is worth remembering in connection with our main theme of the Motor Car Division. You see, many—including the Company's catalogue copywriters at times—attach to the Rolls-Royce such labels as 'craftsmanlike beauty of design, silence, and the constant pursuit of an ideal'. Such a dilettante description denigrates the determination and forceful policy often necessary in this quest not only for perfection but for profitable production, and this brings us to the wartime story of Hs.

Thousands of men and women were working long shifts at

Derby and Crewe. Engine production mushroomed from 600 (four different types) in 1938, to over 12,000 (29 types) at a crucial period of the war, and this explosive expansion was possible because Hs not only said 'Work till it hurts' to his workers but also worked that way himself. Bureaucratic irritations such as war stresses always throw up between government departments and industry—ever since the Lloyd George and Northcliffe shell quarrel of the First World War—were rife, but despite bombing and human strain, Rolls-Royce kept faith. Then, with the coming desert campaigns ahead, the government needed more tanks.

Lord Beaverbrook and Hs had a secret meeting at the Thames House headquarters of The Beaver's personal production unit, and Hs was asked if he could supply Meteor tank engines on a large scale.

He put the position frankly. The firm was already doing a colossal task in meeting the ever-growing demand for Merlin, and when The Beaver countered this in his well-known brusque fashion, Hs was just as blunt.

'If you want those Meteors,' he said, 'Rolls-Royce will need £1,000,000 placed to their credit, and no interference.' It was a Churchillian retort, and no doubt Churchill considered it. On his return through the night to Derby, Hs probably wondered what discussions were proceeding in Whitehall, but next morning came the characteristic Beaver telegram: '*Hives, Rolls-Royce, Derby. The British Government has given you an open credit of one million pounds.*'

As Rolls-Royce jets now dominate the skies, and one day, perhaps sooner than many suppose, the miniature gas-turbine may be applied to the Rolls-Royce car, it must be put on record that jet propulsion was nothing new to Rolls-Royce. Since 1939 a team of designers had been working with Dr. A. A. Griffith, who had joined R.-R. from the Royal Aircraft Establishment, Farnborough. Griffith's ideas were more advanced than Whittle's, but they presented difficulties which could not be speedily solved. Whittle had designed a simple gas-turbine engine which had its first flight in May, 1941. Rovers undertook its manufacture for Power Jets at Barnoldswick and Clitheroe, but this was a strange, new work, full of problems. The Rolls-Royce men believed that in battling with their own technical troubles they had found a way around some of the snags holding up production of the Whittle jet.

Hs's offer was accepted. 'We have frequently advocated to the Ministry', Whittle wrote to him, 'that if any other firm were to be asked to do such a thing it should be Rolls-Royce . . . the only people who have a technical staff sufficiently competent for the purpose.' Out of an exchange between the Rover Company and Rolls-Royce (Rovers took over the tank engine, and Rolls-Royce went ahead with the W2B/23 Rover jet) came the Rolls-Royce Welland, the first of the 'River'-class engines. The Welland powered the Meteor fighter aircraft, and was the first jet engine in the world to be produced in quantity.

Ev (H. I. F. Evernden, MBE) is another who, like Hs, was a living link between the cars of the present day and the era of R himself. He joined R.-R. in 1916 as a designer in the Madsen automatic rifle department, for 30s. a week, and after a period with airship-engine design (including Hawks for the North Sea airships) was transferred to the car division. In April, 1921, he went to West Wittering as a member of Henry Royce's personal staff (R was forced to move back to a house on the Sussex coast from his own Riviera retreat during the First War), and worked with a team including Day and Hardy which was engaged on a task expected to occupy three weeks. In fact Ev remained until R's death in 1933, and helped to design many of the historic pre-war cars including the New Phantom, and the 20, 20/25 and 30-hp cars of the series which through the years has grown to the Silver Wraith and Silver Cloud, as is told in Chapter Four.

When the Second War came, Ev formed in a squash court in W. A. Robotham's house in Duffield, near Derby, a team of 'old hands' and it was Ev who headed the design work of the Meteor tank engines for which the government wrote that open credit of a million pounds. In 1961, after 45 years with the Company, Ev retired, but continued as an independent consultant to Rolls-Royce. His knowledge was of immense value, and we benefit from it still every time we drive any model of a Royce, because not only did he head the design teams for the Silver Wraith and the Bentley Mk VI and Continental, but was the Company's chief advocate for the introduction of automatic transmission and torque converters. This interest began in 1943 when he was appointed a member of Oliver Lucas' government team to the United States to study American tank development, and during this time he became particularly interested in hydraulic torque conversion systems and automatic transmissions, which experience was later applicable to the cars.

Ev was among the first to bridge the Atlantic gap, in a way which subsequent Rolls-Royce enthusiasts have not been able to do. I recall a humorous column by Barry Mather in the *Vancouver Sun* dealing with a 1949 Silver Wraith at a local auction.

' "*Titled Original Owner*," the ad. said. "Does he go with the car?" a man smirked. Yet you sensed he was a Rolls lover, too, jesting uneasily as in church. "What kind is that?" some ignoramus up front asked. "It's a Royals Rice," another told him.

' "A car like that," I remarked, in the tone of one who suggests that it would be sensible economy to buy a Rolls, "a car like that would last you all your life."

' "Yes," my friend said, "but you wouldn't live long enough." '

Three

CREWE

THERE are those, as we have seen, who still mistakenly speak of a Royals Rice. Although Britain's first motoring monarch, Edward VII, drove on the highway in (more accurately, on) an early Daimler, and most Royal motoring in the days of George V and Queen Mary was also in Daimlers, in the present age the Royal link with Rolls-Royce is strong.

So on walking through the huge 1,050-ft long main shop at Crewe in the high summer of 1962, on the occasion of the visit of HRH Princess Margaret and the Earl of Snowdon, I found it surprising that this was the first Royal visit to Rolls-Royce for 22 years. Their Majesties King George VI and Queen Elizabeth were at Derby in 1940.

Princess Margaret, after being received by Lord Leverhulme, Lord-Lieutenant of Cheshire, Sir Denning Pearson (chief executive and deputy chairman at the time), Dr. Llewellyn Smith and other directors and officials, made an hour's tour. With the Earl, she chatted to machine-setters at auto twin milling machines, toured the gear-machining section and the crankshaft line and watched chassis under construction. They saw axle assemblies, brake assemblies, engines, suspension and heating and ventilating systems. In the Trim shop they handled rich hides, watched the carpet machinists, coach-trimmers and body-workers.

They inspected an engine-assembly line, the Royal visitors saw V-8 engines and automatic transmissions being matched, and waited while the first section of an endurance test was given to an engine, simulating a complete journey including stops and gradients. They inspected the Rolls-Royce furnaces and asked the furnaceman about the carbons used, while peering in at the inferno through a sheet of dark, armoured glass; then they watched a demonstration of the detection of hidden faults by X-ray before making a visit to the new paint shop. Here car bodies on overhead conveyors were going through the several dipping processes which precede transfer to floor conveyors for washing, rubbing down and to the application of colour.

During this tour, similar to that which any serious student of engineering can make to the Rolls-Royce Motor Car Division by special invitation from the Crewe directorate, I kept recalling that it was then just 24 years since a handful of Rolls-Royce men studied a pleasant stretch of grassland on the outskirts of Crewe, took off their jackets to help the farmer get in a crop of hay, and then tackled a tough and urgent job, setting up the Crewe factory to help meet the demand for Merlin engines.

Brunt of the burden to create this new production centre where the cars are now built fell on the men from Derby. There was John Morris, first manager of the factory; Dick Garner, later to become material manager at Crewe; Ted Glover, later technical assistant to the general works manager; Bill Ward; Jack Valentine, later plant and equipment engineer; Ron Dyson, training superintendent, and Wilson Elliott who became deputy to Sid Torr as plant and equipment engineer. These are the men who formed the advance party that went from Derby all those years ago. Twenty-five years later, when Crewe was celebrating its first quarter-century, only two at the factory could date their service back to before July, 1938, apart from those ex-Derby men who helped to build the place. A dozen had signed on for work at Crewe by the August, and from then onwards the labour force increased rapidly.

Sid Torr, one of the two 'oldest' Crewe employees, started working on 11th July, 1938, as a plant draughtsman, using temporary offices at Imperial Chambers. 'The weather was atrocious and the site a sea of mud,' he told me. 'A sleeper road had to be laid down. But the contractors did a fine job and by mid-October the erection of the factory was sufficiently advanced to enable 400 ft of the main workshop to be partitioned off, and the first machines installed.'

As the machines were ready, so also were the men. Training facilities were set up in the big Co-operative garage in Crewe's Middlewich Street, and here fitters and some machinists were trained. Jim Dennison, later to become an inspector on the chassis line, told me how two Merlin engines were used to train the fitters. 'These engines were repeatedly taken to pieces and put together again, under the direction of Jack Acheson' (an ex-Derby man, to become in time fitting foreman), 'and I recall we had a uniform then: brown overalls with a red collar.' At the time of the 25th celebrations, I discovered that Geoff Leach was among the August, 1938, newcomers taken on as testers, and as they had not done this work before they were sent first to Derby to learn the work at Sinfin. Twenty-five years later, Leach was a charge-hand fitter and had remained at the work all the time. 'I've tested pretty well everything that we have produced here,' he said, 'and I still wouldn't change the job for any other.'

Crewe's war record—a peak labour force of some 10,000 and an engine output of around 200 a week—is well remembered. And although the immediate post-war run-down hurt Crewe, the fact is that as a result of post-war building—the gear shop is an example—Rolls-Royce today occupies a bigger area at Crewe than during the war. This is one measure of the Motor Car Division's achievements. It was not an easy change-over. Men had to apply their skills to new fields, some had to learn new skills. Even an official Rolls-Royce historian noted: 'They showed their adaptability. Motor car production was quite new to the factory, and this was no ordinary car!'

Rolls-Royce do keep their people. To be apprenticed to Rolls-Royce is to attend the best engineering university in the United Kingdom. Looking through the staff records a year or two ago when there were 84,377 men and women on the payroll, the average length of service was 10·8 years. Over 15,000 people had worked for R.-R. for up to 14 years, nearly a thousand had between 25 and 39 years' service, and 622 could claim service of 40 years and over. They, too, knew the origins of the Royce tradition. When you visit Crewe, if you merit the friendship of one of the old-time craftsmen you may be fortunate enough to find yourself in the Valentine Pavilion, which typifies the com-radeship of those who are Rolls-Royce. Back in 1938, JV (J. Valentine) started a section known as Crewe Welfare. After 1952 he was a trustee of Rolls-Royce Welfare Trust. JV believed the growing army of Crewe workers must have relaxation, during the Munich-time stress, at the height of war, and of course during the difficult years of the Motor Car Division after 1945. Relaxation means sport. Sport means a pavilion. There was none at Crewe, so JV badgered the Crewe section of the Rolls-Royce Welfare Amenities Society, and scrounged the first small pavilion—a contractor's wooden hut on the factory site when the factory was being built. Today the Valentine Pavilion, perhaps the finest in the entire Rolls-Royce organisation, is the realisation of a dream. The Company donated the ground, a large air-conditioned building with kitchens, lounges and billiards rooms has been built. Surrounding it are 6,000 roses, and a thousand shrubs. Unless one is on the Crewe payroll, to get an invitation to the Valentine Pavilion is an honour indeed. And if you are also invited to tour the car works at Crewe, what is to be seen?

The story runs that Royce once opined to his friend Eric Gill that 'Whatever is rightly done, however humble, is noble.' Personally I have always doubted the way the story is told, for Royce was a man usually given to brusque comments such as 'I can do simple arithmetic' to those who mentioned slide-rule calculations, and 'I'm just a mechanic' to those who flattered the engineering beauty of his designs. However, either Gill or Royce had this theme of 'Whatever is rightly done' in mind, and Gill himself carved it in stone over the mantelpiece of the main room of R's house at West Wittering, in the same style of lettering Gill used for the 'Nation Shall Speak Peace Unto Nation' legend over the BBC's Broadcasting House in London. With R's legend, however, it was done in Latin, a subject R did not take in the early days of his self-acquired education. Nevertheless *Quidvis recte factum: quamvis humile praeclarum* it is, and today this is the legend which greets the visitor to Crewe. It is on a shield in the austere entrance to the Motor Car Division.

While this greeting is in a dead language, everything else at Crewe is living, modern, forward-looking: and the same is true of Clan Foundry, Belper, about 10 miles from Derby, where a good deal of the original design, testing and research has been done since 1946. Visitors from the United States, knowing that the system of automatic transmission used in the cars is developed from an established design, somehow seem to expect to find big crates labelled 'General Motors Detroit' in the loading bays at Crewe, with US-built transmissions being bolted direct to R.-R. built motors. However, the automatic transmission system is unique, developed *from* the American prototype, and not only do Rolls-Royce make it complete, but even their own nuts and bolts. I mention this to show that a first visit to Crewe is different from what many people expect.

Although the main assembly hall is over a thousand feet long, the Car Division makes no claim to big statistics. Total produc-

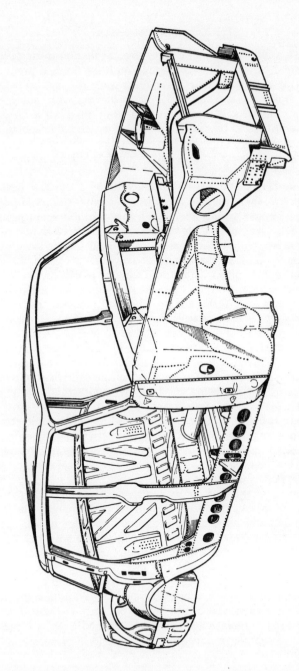

Three-quarter view of body shell of the standard Silver Shadow 4-door saloon

tion is often less than 2,000 cars a year, so manufacturing and development costs are thickly spread. With the finished product so glittering as a diamond, you might expect the factory to be one of those you-can-eat-off-the-floor places, with walls of gleaming white tiles. It is not. There is more tiling in the Gents' than around the car production line. Rather, the atmosphere is that of a huge, well-appointed service-station, with odd factory and workshop corners where a surprisingly high proportion of hand processes are carried out.

The number of bought-out components on a modern Rolls-Royce is less than that of most other manufacturers. Lucas electrics, of course. Sub-frames, sub-frame assemblies and pressings by John Thompson Motor Pressings, of Wolverhampton. (This firm has supplied chassis frames of Rolls-Royce since the Silver Ghost of 1909.) Hardy Spicer (Birfield) propeller shafts. Champion spark plugs. Marston radiator blocks. Avon and Dunlop tyres. John Morgan (Jemca) sun visors. And a handful of similar specialist firms are on the Rolls-Royce 'By royal command' list. But no matter how carefully these accessories are designed and built, the men at Crewe test every one (not merely a sample batch), and they have designed their own rigs for these factory checks. You will see starter-motors, dynamos and AC generators, automatic-choke mechanisms, thermostats and power-steering pumps being checked. Even with routine equipment such as electrical accessories, these are made by outside suppliers to Rolls-Royce specifications, and modern manufacturing and servicing philosophy proves this is better (but not always cheaper) than in the days when Royce wound his own dynamos —and indeed made at Derby *all* the major electrical equipment except the headlamps and the battery.

With some suspension components, electronic recording instruments automatically draw graphs of performance, and at various points this information is actually recorded on the car. It was Ronald Barker in *Autocar*, for example, who noted that every rear axle road spring has its actual poundage, free camber, loaded camber and serial number recorded on a plate on its gaiter: and that 'On the reverse side of every wooden panel are the part and log numbers: if one picnic table, say, is damaged in a car in the United States, the owner has only to quote these references and a replacement will be prepared from a veneer *from the same log*, since a portion of each is held in storage.'

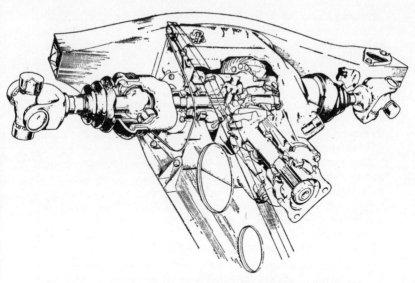

Cut-away perspective drawing of rear transmission assembly
of the Silver Shadow, with independent rear suspension

Avery dynamic-balancing machines are used with each of the
moving components of engine and gearbox. Tiny balance plates
are added to the transmission, and metal is drilled from the
damper flange to obtain good ending dynamic balancing.
Crankshafts are produced with extreme care, and the average
daily production is only five; one reason for this comparatively
slow output is that a test piece of the forged EN 19 steel for
each crankshaft is first given a check in the metallurgical laboratory at Crewe before any machining is done on the shaft. This
steel is heat-treated to a Brinell hardness of a maximum of 286.
One or two modern design features help in production of components such as crankshafts. For example, all the preceding
Rolls-Royce engines (including the eight-cylinder Phantom IV's)
had bored out crankpins and main bearings to provide sludge
traps. When the V-8 engine was on the drawing-board it was
felt that the weight of the sludge in a unit of these dimensions
might result in a rotating couple greater than 70 lb/ft, so there
are no sludge traps in the V-8, and therefore a slight reduction
in complexity as this part of the drilling and machining is un-

necessary. It is most interesting to see how the Crewe engine teams dynamically balance each crankshaft by removing excess material from the balance weights after final grinding. Another detail which helps to produce that Rolls-Royce smoothness is the balancing of connecting rods. There are tiny balancing pads on the extremities of the rods themselves, and these are machined to the extent necessary to bring the reciprocating and rotating weights to the designed limits, the tolerance being only $\pm$ 8 drams reciprocating and $\pm$ 4 drams rotating for a *pair* of rods. (There are 16 drams to the ounce.)

Design and craftsmanship go hand in hand as each component of the engine is assembled. For example, watch the connecting rods being bolted in place, with no possibility of the bolts rotating and working loose. Says Mr. A. J. Phillips, the senior member of the design team of the Rolls-Royce V-8 engine: 'Many of the better-known methods were tried and discarded as being either difficult to make or conducive to "stress-raisers" before the final design was evolved. On a raised diameter of the bolt a parallel knurl is provided in a longitudinal position such that when it is forced into a mating bore the resulting scoring of the hole is situated near the neutral axis of the rod-half of the cap. After a small modification this system worked well and gave a nicely-proportioned bolt bead which is easily produced. The Brinell hardness of bolt and rod are similar, approaching 300, and rolled threads are used. No special locking device is provided on the nuts, although almost 10 years of running on experimental cars was needed before confidence was sufficient to take this step!'

During assembly at Crewe partially complete engines are shifted from one section to another on rollers. As one watches assembly, the ingenious design which produces the great rigidity of the crankcase is obvious. In many vital details manufacturing techniques differ from those of other engine-builders. The threads in the block are standard UNF truncated, and the holes for the female thread are tapped under size. Although in one sense the whole power unit is made regardless of expense, Crewe obviously does not go looking for trouble. For example, some designers suggested light alloy connecting rods with forged steel caps, and these do give very satisfactory results on some other designs. However, Rolls-Royce still keep to steel connecting rods since a difficulty with forged-steel caps in aluminium rods is in the initial machining, and it can make a difficult production problem.

In assembling the engine oil pumps great care is taken; the current design uses bronze and steel gears running together. (In an in-line engine, Mr. Phillips told me, he had actually seen a pair of steel skew gears sparking under oil.) A special bronze is used for the appropriate skew gear in the present pumps, and a fairly heavy wear occurs during running-in, but after initial break-in no further wear is apparent. Each pump is tested to give 40 lb/sq. in. when running at normal operational speed, and a flow not less than 86 pints per minute. Coolant pumps are similarly tested to give a flow of 40 gallons per minute at 20 lb/sq. in.

Because of the current Detroit interest in close-cored cast iron engines, American visitors to Crewe frequently ask questions about manufacturing problems of an engine such as that in the Silver Shadow which has a fine power-weight showing. The current series gives 40 bhp/l. But inevitably the men at Crewe are asked if they will follow the Detroit trend. Some time ago when Mr. Phillips was asked this same question. His frank answer then was: 'If I could get cast iron as light as aluminium, I would prefer it, because aluminium is a difficult material to work with: moreover, American manufacturers are very clever at iron casting. They seem to be able to get a cast-iron manifold which has a section thickness of 80 thou. Britain does not seem to be able to get Lake iron, and consequently our ironfounders say that sections must be at least $\frac{3}{16}$ in. We seem to be able to cast aluminium a whole lot better in Great Britain, possibly because there is a greater fund of experience in the use of light alloys.'

It is perhaps unfair to take Mr. Phillips' reply out of context, and anyway this view was expressed, as I say, some time ago. There is continuing research at Rolls-Royce, and when another engineer asked if, having the opportunity to conduct the same exercise again, would Mr. Phillips design the engine differently, his answer was a blunt No, except for minor details. 'The usual considerations would be given to seeing if the job could be produced better technically and more cheaply,' he elaborated. 'But aluminium, with all its failings, must be used if a light-weight power unit is to be produced.'

As some models of the car sell overseas for more than $20,000 a familiar query from distant visitors to Crewe is on the subject of tests-to-destruction. Sadists have a mental picture of development engineers of this enormously wealthy Company crashing costly cars regardless of expense! What is far more important from the engineering point of view is the test-to-destruction of components, and even of nuts and bolts. The men at Crewe are sometimes asked whether, before specifying a torque load on any particular specification, they test (say) the bolt in question to failure, to determine the breaking load. The official reply is that Rolls-Royce torque-load every normally stressed bolt on the engine to a standardised figure; and in case of heavily-loaded bolts such as big-end bolts, the torque loading is arrived at experimentally by measuring the bolt stretch during the development period of running, and it is usual to stress these up to a figure very near to the yield-point of the material.

Advent of comparatively new materials such as high-grade fibreglass has enabled Crewe to evolve its own techniques. Manufacture of fibreglass components is largely women's work, two of the present members of this section having come to R.-R. from a clothing factory and from the fitting-shops of the locomotive works at Crewe respectively. Normally a team of two or three is adequate for the production of fibreglass components for the Motor Car Division. Stoneguards, air-silencers and similar components are now made from fibreglass, and for certain specific purposes the material is better than steel or wood, being lighter, tougher, and having sound-deadening properties.

Moulds in which these components are made are first coated with wax, then a thin layer of 'mix' is poured in or laid on with a brush, and over that goes a layer of glass fibre of a specified thickness. Further 'mix' and fibre are added to build up the necessary thickness. To get a firm job the fibre has to be properly impregnated with the mix, and then with care the components can be removed from the mould within half an hour.

An interesting manufacturing process is to be seen at Crewe's Aero Shop Austenal foundry, where by 'lost-wax' techniques parts have been made ranging from the Spirit of Ecstasy (Flying Lady) mascot, to nozzle guide vanes for jet engines. This is a very old process, used centuries ago by craftsmen producing hollow bronze statues and items of that kind. Essentially, a wax duplicate of the object to be cast is made and surrounded by plaster or some similar refractory material. When this is set, the wax is melted out to leave the hollow into which the casting metal is then poured. Finally, of course, the outer part of the mould is chipped off. While not a process ideally suited for mass-production methods, it is one with distinct advantages for manufacture of high-detail or precision items such as those on the Rolls-Royce list. It was used right from the inception of the radiator mascot in February, 1911.

Crewe's Austenal foundry began in 1956 as an experimental unit housed in a small shed, making car mascots and trying out various techniques of manufacture of specialised aero engine components; by 1958 it was an integral part of the Aero Shop, and ways had been found of mechanising some of the operations. In place of the centuries-old plaster, Crewe now use what they term an investing mixture, or slurry. Its exact composition is secret, but some of the constituents include sodium silicate and nitric acid. Patterns ready for casting are assembled in batches and put into an automatic vibration machine, the only one of its kind in the country, built to Crewe's own design. Then with the slurry ready to be packed down, the operator touches a pedal and a measured quantity of melted wax is spread over the mould containers, known as flasks. Despite scientific aids and a certain degree of automation, only 18 flasks can be filled at a time, and such is the delicacy of the process that it takes 16 hours for the wax to be melted from each batch.

After firing, the mould is ready for casting, and a pre-weighed quantity of metal is melted in a small furnace under strict temperature control; the exact temperature is continuously recorded on a thermograph chart. At a pre-determined instant, the furnace is inverted, and the molten metal runs into the mould. When the casting has cooled, most of the refractory is broken off, and all castings are loaded into a Tilghman's Wheelabrator, in which at a certain period of the cycle the items are sandblasted. Some of the silica used comes, in fact, from preceding batches of chipped-off refractory, and by adding a quantity of crushed shell to this several times a week it produces the correct degree of abrasiveness.

The present series of Spirit of Ecstasy mascots is made from a special stainless steel, but the design is still fundamentally that of the distinguished Edwardian artist Charles Sykes, RA, who, impressed by a drive in a Silver Ghost with Lord Montagu of Beaulieu, had some discussion on the subject of the car's silence, power, grace and speed. The outcome was that Montagu introduced Charles Sykes to Claude Johnson, by then the managing director of Rolls-Royce Ltd. The outcome of this meeting was the original form of the mascot which in one design or another now almost without exception graces the radiator-shell of the car.

As car mascots are rare these days, it is worth noting why the Company commissioned Charles Sykes to sculpt this unique statuette. 'The directors of Rolls-Royce Ltd.', they announced in March, 1911, 'have always taken pride in endeavouring to ensure that the outward appearance of the Rolls-Royce chassis shall be as beautiful as possible. Purity in outline and a general appearance of elegance have in this respect been their ideals. Naturally, therefore, the directors of Rolls-Royce Ltd. were somehat appalled in noticing that a few owners of Rolls-Royce cars attached to the water caps of the radiators very grotesque forms of mascots, such as gollywogs, policemen, and black cats. It seemed to them that if a mascot were designed by an owner it might be possible to provide one of some beauty, and they therefore commissioned Mr. Charles Sykes to prepare a model of one which should convey the spirit of the Rolls-Royce, namely, speed with silence, absence of vibration, the mysterious harnessing of great energy, a beautiful living organism of superb grace, like a sailing yacht. Such is the spirit of the Rolls-Royce, and such is the combination of virtues which Mr. Charles Sykes has expressed so admirably in the graceful little lady, who is designed as the figurehead of the Rolls-Royce.

'The artist explains that in the designing of this graceful little goddess he had in mind the spirit of ecstasy who has selected road travel as her supreme delight, and has alighted on the prow of a Rolls-Royce car to revel in the freshness of the air and the musical sound of her fluttering draperies. She is expressing her keen enjoyment, with arms outstretched and her sight fixed upon the distance.'

This statement, which one may feel was a fulsome one to come from the Company in that formal era, sums up not only the Spirit of Ecstasy but also the essential meaning of Rolls-Royce motoring itself.

Charles Sykes designed a number of other beautiful objects of classic motoring interest, including the magnificent gilt trophy presented for the Second Montagu Cup Trophy of 1908, won by Frank Newton in a Napier. He had the gift of seeing the

Rolls-Royce were the first British car manufacturers to have their own drop forge. Forging of experimental parts is still done here, with a two ton steam hammer for hand-forging. Typical of Rolls-Royce loyal craft tradition is that exemplified by Mr. Probert seen inspecting the work. He had been superintendent of this department since its creation in 1916

Above Stripped chassis of a Silver Dawn waiting to be put through test. This model was first introduced in 1949, with 4,257 cc engine and four-speed manual box. In 1951 capacity was increased to 4,566 cc, and the automatic transmission seen here was adopted

Below A section of the Engine Test Department at Derby, the Works designed by Sir Henry Royce, opened in 1908. This is a scene of the 1920's, and the engine on test is one of the 3,127 cc 20 hp power-units first introduced in 1922, with the three-speed centre-change gearbox

artistic aspects of automobilism, and was commissioned by the Company to undertake a series of paintings illustrating the Silver Ghost in a variety of country settings. One of these, an Edwardian sporting scene of guns, dated 1910, is reproduced in my *Book of the Silver Ghost*, and interestingly this painting was completed months prior to the production of the first Spirit of Ecstasy mascot. Sykes shows an upright figure, devoid of sufficient detail to tell is whether by then he had the Spirit in mind.

To the irreverent among Rolls-Royce owners the mascot is sometimes known as Emily, or 'Miss Thornton in her flowing nightie', following reports that Sykes had used Miss Eleanor Thornton, the gracious and attractive personal assistant to the first Lord Montagu. One of the original 22-in. statuettes is in the Beaulieu collection, and possibly by exercising some artistic licence one can find a facial resemblance with Miss Thornton. Charles Sykes' daughter Jo (Mrs. Phillips) was closely connected with the production of the mascots until 1940, and says there were a number of women who modelled for the Spirit in her father's studio.

A rather unusual agreement was drawn up between Mr. Sykes and the Company, who wanted the original designer to be responsible so far as possible for perfect productions as hand-made works of art. The 1911 Company announcement informed new owners that: 'Arrangements are being made by which an owner of a Rolls-Royce car may acquire one of these figureheads at a cost of a few pounds.' The pre-war price was between four and six guineas. From 1911 until 1928 every Rolls-Royce mascot produced was personally checked by Mr. Sykes, who had a small staff of experts for this special work. His artistic assistant Miss Bond helped to check detail work of the lost-wax castings prior to plating, and the first foundryman was an Italian artist Angeloni. On his death the foundry work was taken over by a Jersey craftsman Lemonnier. By 1928 Mr. Sykes needed to be relieved of much of the responsibility because of the pressures resulting from his successful career, so Jo Sykes took over mascot production until the outbreak of war. Charles Sykes died in 1950, just two years after Crewe had gone into production with the latest form of the Spirit of Ecstasy, using stainless steel and recently developed precision casting techniques.

One of the Rolls-Royce legends which lives on, like the 'solid gold horn button', is that the Flying Lady is of solid silver.

Several different alloys have been used, and within recent years Crewe has changed the stainless steel content, but silver has never been used. The very first Spirits were of white-metal, then of a copper-zinc-tin alloy somewhat similar to German silver, while for a time the mascots were of nickel, which did not entail plating. Most of the chromium-plated Spirits are castings of a copper-zinc alloy, nickel-plated, while a few to special order have been silver- or even gold-plated. The kneeling figure was modelled by Mr. Sykes in 1933, and supplied to the Company under a new agreement drawn up on 26th January, 1934, following an experimental design of a smaller 5-in. winged mascot the purpose of which, like the kneeler, is to clear the bonnet (hood) sides when the engine compartment is opened. The kneeling Spirit is used on the Silver Wraith and Dawn models, but a smaller edition of the upright figure was introduced in April, 1955, for the Silver Cloud 1, and continued at Crewe for the Phantom V and the Silver Shadow; in the latest series the hood opening of the monocoque body does not demand the restrained proportions of the kneeling Spirit.

Among the few variations on the Sykes' Spirit of Ecstasy theme is the mascot which Crewe provided for Her Majesty the Queen, first remarked by Rolls-Royce enthusiasts when it appeared on the State Phantom IV. The figure is that of St. George slaying the Dragon, and because of the delicate sculpting had to be subjected to vibration tests. Structural weaknesses came to light, and a Crewe artist modified the design before this exclusive Royal mascot was supplied.

Rolls-Royce used to make their own valve springs at Derby, but today the aero-engine division in Scotland at Hillington is the only spring making section in the Company; indeed it is one of the few hand-craft jobs in the Aero Division.

At Hillington springs are made from five different wires for a hundred different purposes, and the grades currently used include hard carbon steel, chrome vanadium, hard stainless steel, and two nimonics. Coiling is done by hand and also by machine, and there are electronic checks on diameter limits and on poundage. Hand-craft techniques are still employed for grinding spring ends, squaring, and for adjusting free length. According to the purpose the spring has to do, grinding, de-burring, chamfering, clipping, heat-treatment, blasting, plating or enamelling follow. And when you ask the men in the Spring shop if all this special care is justified, they will tell you that a piston-engine valve spring should go up and down more than 86 million times before it tires.

Crewe can call on the resources of every other section in the Company, and while Hillington's springs are perhaps routine examples, there is something of unique interest to be seen at the Rolls-Royce Ghyll Brow factory near Barnoldswick. This is the largest high-voltage electron beam welding machine in Britain. It can weld 2-in.-thick stainless steel at a speed of 4 in. a minute, or, at the other end of the scale, aluminium alloy only 0·005 in. thick at the rate of 120 in./min.

Electron beam welding uses tube somewhat in principle to the cathode-ray tube of a television receiver. Electrons from a heated cathode are accelerated by EHT to about half the speed of light, then concentrated into a fine beam only a few thousandths of an inch in diameter but with a power intensity more than 5,000 times greater than a conventional arc. This beam is precisely controlled down to the workpiece with a viewing system which in effect looks down the beam itself. The impact of the electrons on the metal melts the material over a minute area, and the energy of the beam generates heat right through the joint. Moving the workpiece or deflecting the beam (as in television) enables a continuous weld to be produced. As normally no additional material such as welding wire is needed, this obviates any need to prepare the workpiece by forming chamfers or grooves. Moreover, the weld is made in one pass instead of having to be built up in layers.

Unlike arc welding, the whole process is carried out in a chamber evacuated to an extremely high degree. Just how near completion is the degree of evacuation can be appreciated from the fact that while the standard atmospheric pressure is 760 mm of mercury, when the chamber is ready for welding, the reading is one-tenth of one thousandth of a millimetre of mercury. At this extremely low pressure the molecules in the chamber are so widely spread that they do not interfere with the gun's electron beam, so the result is an absolutely metallurgically pure weld, free from contamination.

The first high-voltage beam welding machine to be brought into the United Kingdom was installed at Ghyll Brow in 1961. This machine, made by the Carl Zeiss Foundation in West Germany, had a beam power of 3 kilowatts and a vacuum chamber

1 ft 6 in. long. It was used for experiments on the application of this technique, and was later fitted with a chamber 3 ft long. A later machine, with a 6 kilowatt gun and a vacuum chamber 14 ft long, was built for Rolls-Royce by Hawker Siddeley Dynamics at Hatfield. Some American visitors to the factory are familiar with the system, because in 1959 the Hamilton Standard Company in the United States acquired rights to manufacture the Zeiss machine, and in 1964 Hawker Siddeley Dynamics took a licence from Hamilton Standard to manufacture in Great Britain.

Another advanced piece of equipment the visitor to the Motor Car Division finds in use is the Muirhead automatic recording wave analyser, which has become a permanent feature of the Division's Electronics and Vibration laboratory. Some years ago Rolls-Royce installed in the Motor Car Division a central recording system connected by land-lines to the test-bed, experimental garage and rig shop. When first installed, a manually operated Muirhead Pametrada wave analyser formed a part of the system, and was used for noise investigation, the measurement of torsional vibrations and engine and car roughness. It became obvious that the work could be divided into main groups, one needing the attention of a highly skilled operative, and the other which is routine and could be carried out by some form of automatic machine. The early Muirhead analyser was motorised experimentally, but eventually Muirheads produced the K-100 automatic wave recording analyser (later superseded by the K-101) which is now installed in the Motor Car Division's central recording room.

Mr. J. C. Coyle, physicist in charge of this important Rolls-Royce laboratory, has devised interesting new techniques for measurement of noise and vibration in vehicles. The usual practice when taking these measurements was to record the noise for a number of seconds on a high-fidelity scientific tape-recorder while the car is passing over a test track. This tape is then made into a continuous loop and played back into the analyser in the laboratory. The amplitude of the recorded noise fluctuates rapidly because of the random excitation the car receives from the road surface via the tyres and suspension, and the technician is faced with the difficulty of deciding what reading he will take for his answer, while the needle of the meter on his wave analyser dances from one end of the scale to the other.

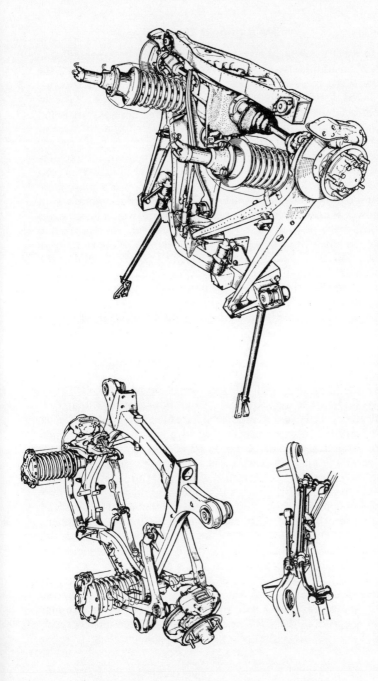

Front and rear sub-frame and suspension assemblies of the Silver Shadow. The two diagrams at the left show the layout at the front, the diagram on the right illustrating the rear assembly with torque reaction arm and the two suspension cross-member links (radius rods)

In early experiments it was found, as might be expected, that when an amplitude/frequency recorder was used to print, the value it recorded was the peak value of the noise the microphone detected during any one run, and of course this can produce an incorrect impression. In a number of Crewe tests it was found that quite large differences in noise levels were apparent, and at 80 c/s the level varies by as much as 8 dB. Large peaks are caused by loose stones from the road coming in contact with the underside of the body, and from the laboratory point of view these can be neglected. Crewe have arrived scientifically at a reasonable average peak value, and it is found that most of the noise which might prove objectionable in a car of the Rolls-Royce type ranges in frequency from about 30 to 500 c/s, and an analysis can be made in approximately $2\frac{1}{2}$ minutes, largely due to the techniques evolved by Mr. Coyle and to the high degree of precision of the Muirhead automatic recording wave analyser.

After getting this detailed picture of the noise spectrum in a car, the engineer is next faced with the problem of producing an end product quiet enough to be acceptable with regard to the high Rolls-Royce standard, of which it jokingly used to be said: 'The loudest noise you hear at 60 is the ticking of the clock.' (Nowadays the main source of noise is not the clock, but the tyres.)

In the laboratory you will see a large rig which Rolls-Royce have built up to reproduce test conditions for each material. This rig is on a base of a large steel plate of sufficient weight never to be critically acoustically damped by any test material applied to it, and this assembly is tuned to vibrate at its fundamental mode at 150 c/s by a powerful electromagnet. Pressure fluctuations produced by the vibration of the plate are converted into an electrical signal through a microphone, and when the power to the magnet is switched off, the decay of the signal is measured with respect to time. One method used by the research teams is to photograph the decay of the signal as it appears on the screen of the oscilloscope, and it has been found convenient in certain laboratory techniques to use a camera with an oscilloscope lens and a Polaroid Land back. Photographs of waveform traces can be taken with the standard 3,000-ASA film packs with an exposure of 100th sec at f/16, where the maximum writing-speed of the CRT exceeds 3,500 cm per microsecond; and for other tests the 10,000-ASA PolaScope stock is used.

This has a writing rate twice as fast as that of the 3,000-speed film, and can give a photographic recording of pulses with rise-times in the sub-nanosecond range.

At Crewe it is fascinating to see engines being put through development work in this way, a phase of the Motor Car Division's activities which is not open to the general public. Much engine development work involves measurement of torsional vibrations in the crankshaft, and these measurements are made at Rolls-Royce using an inductive torsiograph in conjunction with a frequency-modulated system, the output of which is fed into the Muirhead wave analyser. It is almost an automatic process, completed by the engine operator without the need for any assistance from an electronic technician.

What the operator customarily does is to observe how the overall amplitude of the vibrations varies with the speed, and afterwards to examine the peaks in more detail for their frequency and amplitude components. In this way it can be discovered the speeds at which resonance of the crankshaft will occur. When the engine has been set to one of these pre-determined speeds, the analyser is started remotely by the tester. A change of speed is indicated to him automatically when the analyser has completed its programme, a pair of contacts closing to illuminate a signal lamp. In this way Crewe can carry out a complete series of crankshaft torsional vibration tests by one man.

To the non-technical, watching noise-recording tape-machines playing back, Muirhead wave analysers at work, and Polaroid Land delivering 'instant-pictures' photographic results, is fascinating yet not very informative. But, moving on to the body paint shop at Crewe, one sees conveyors, hand-spraying booths and dipping tanks the purpose of which is obvious even to the do-it-yourself home paint-sprayer. Again, however, what really matters, and what produces the Rolls-Royce quality of finish, is generally what is *not* seen. They will tell you in the body paint shop: 'Whilst the highest quality paints are always used, these materials are available and some are used by other car manufacturers. The quality here stems not so much from the materials themselves, but from their handling. Again, there is rigorous inspection carried out after each painting and rubbing down operation.'

Crewe's present highly mechanised paint plant was put into

operation in 1961, and it combines modern production methods with many of the old-time coach-painting techniques. One of the important features of the new plant is the inclusion of a special foundation coat. This takes the form of a water-thinned grey primer. Rolls-Royce were the first British car manufacturers to install this process. The coat is applied by almost immersing the body in paint, and at the same time spraying it with a large number of jets of paint set at different angles. There is, of course, elaborate air-conditioning of all hand-spray booths, systems for carefully controlling temperature under which the many colour coats are sprayed, and the elaborate mixing of all paint used in production in a separate shop, from which the paint is pumped to each booth separately.

Crewe rightly claim that, with at least 60 different stages associated with hand-finished paint work, the result is one of the best-protected and highest-quality bodies in the car industry today. There are four main conveyors, and two separate circuits. Visitors to this section at Crewe see the body shells complete with wings and hood (bonnet) being inspected for any flaws before transfer to Conveyor A, where in a series of transits each body is dipped and sprayed in hot cleaning solution, then dipped and sprayed in cold and later in hot water, dipped and sprayed in phosphate solution, given two dips and sprays with cold water, then sprayed with a de-mineralised water. The body shell is next transferred to Conveyor B and dried in an oven, sprayed with acid-etch primer, dipped in water-thinned grey primer, allowed to drain, and finally baked in an oven. Craftsmen at this stage fill any minute surface imperfections with stopping-putty, and the shell is transferred to Conveyor C.

During its first circuit on this conveyor, it is hand sprayed with brown filler, baked, and all joints on the underside are sealed. On the second circuit the body is hand sprayed with red-oxide filler, baked, hand sprayed with a guide coat- and the underside sprayed with an anti-drum solution. It is now allowed to dry at ambient air temperature for eight hours, and transferred to Conveyor D on which it makes two separate circuits. Here a number of special Crewe techniques come into play, and the whole of the process cannot be disclosed. However, some of the basic processes performed as the shell moves along on its conveyor include rubbing down with abrasive papers, wiping with cloths impregnated with a non-drying varnish to remove dust, spraying

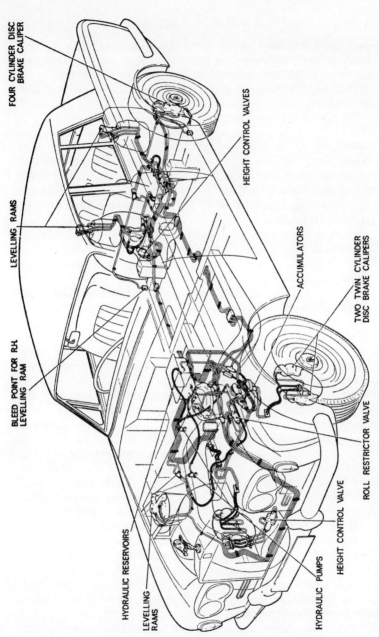

FOUR CYLINDER DISC BRAKE CALIPER

HEIGHT CONTROL VALVES

LEVELLING RAMS

BLEED POINT FOR R.H. LEVELLING RAM

ACCUMULATORS

TWO TWIN CYLINDER DISC BRAKE CALIPERS

ROLL RESTRICTOR VALVE

HEIGHT CONTROL VALVE

HYDRAULIC PUMPS

LEVELLING RAMS

HYDRAULIC RESERVOIRS

Position of hydraulic components on the Silver Shadow

with de-mineralised water, hand spraying with surfacer coat, application of cellulose stopping putty, upper and lower sections (separately) sprayed with colour build-up, air-drying and force-drying. All this helps to give a mirror-like finish, anti-rust and anti-drum.

Another interesting section at Crewe is the Electrical Unit Assembly, where roughly a quarter of a mile of wiring goes into each Rolls-Royce and Bentley. These lengths are made up, as in most other cars, into looms, runs of cable grouped together and colour-coded. The longest is 17 ft, and the most complex is the dashboard (facia panel) loom which contains 49 wires. Some of the assemblers in Electrical Unit Assembly have been working with Rolls-Royce for half a lifetime, and I particularly recall that when I first visited this reorganised Unit in 1958 I chanced to meet a former worker in this section, Florrie Austin. She worked for Royce in the very beginning, at Cooke Street, Manchester. Her job was winding trembler coils for Silver Ghosts and earlier models, using an old sewing-machine table fitted with a spindle and operated by a foot treadle. Today, of course, everything is mechanised, and even the serial numbers of the electrical looms are specified by computer. It is not all merely wiring, of course. This Crewe unit assemble the ventilating and demisting systems, and much of the refrigeration plant. Into the front of the ducting which runs beneath the wing you may see the hot-water matrix being installed, the two-speed fans, the flap-valves controlling the rate at which warm or cool air enters the car. Nowadays, with the complex electrical units on the Silver Shadow, the work of the Assembly shop is intricate, and some engineering innovations are first seen here. They can tell you, for example, the serial numbers of the Silver Cloud on which, a decade ago, a nylon gear was used for the first time in a Rolls-Royce car. It was, in fact, part of the gearing driving the electrically operated chain window lift.

It is wrong, nevertheless, to depict Crewe only as a series of units or cells where old-time craftsmanship goes on, albeit many processes *are* better done by hand, and more economically too, in a factory where car production does not exceed a hundred cars a week. One of the secrets of Crewe's success, to my mind, is the ingenious blending of craft techniques with the ruthless efficiency of the computer.

Visitors to Crewe, seeing so many unit cells with hand operatives, sometimes ask almost apologetically: 'I suppose you don't use a computer . . . ?' The position is that not only does every facet of car design, development and production get checked by a computer, but currently some 25 computer-based major systems are under development throughout the Company, covering everything from cars to missiles, gas-turbines to nuclear submarine plants. Rolls-Royce went into computer planning in a big way in 1965, when they organised a survey with a team of about 90 people, and this produced a 10-year plan. The Computer Centre was started, and data-processing units installed at Derby and in the Scottish group of factories. The future Rolls-Royce plan is for 'polycentric' computing, which means that each minor computer is connected by high-speed data transmission links (some operating via the Post Office Tower in London, and its associated links) to a central, more powerful system which in turn is connected to the central computer complex in Derby.

With typical R.-R. thoroughness the computer chiefs are planning 'terminals' of practical use in the Car Division and elsewhere. As explained by Mr. J. W. Foord, in charge of computer communications: 'The basic philosophy is to design a terminal which has characteristics directly related to the environment in which its user works. It seems pointless to place a typewriter terminal in the Foundry, to be operated by somebody who uses asbestos gloves. If a man is used to turning dials, then we intend to give him a terminal consisting of dials. If he is used to drawing, then we propose to give him a terminal with a "light-pen" facility. We intend to develop the concept of transmitting information as a logical extension of doing the job.'

One might feel that with a car some models of which retail at over £10,000, and jet-engine programmes running into many millions, the cost of all this would not matter. It does. Says Mr. L. Griffiths, chief computing engineer of Rolls-Royce Ltd.: 'The investment required makes it imperative to obtain an outstanding return.'

Among the many legends of Crewe there is some truth in the story the Company buys outstanding cars by other makers, dissects them, studies the design of every component and puts them all through their own tests for comparison. And at Crewe they have a masterly gift of improvisation. Bits of Rolls-Royce cars and others are used to build up improvised test-rigs, some of Heath Robinson appearance but of utmost utility. An example is a strange trailer which the residents of Crewe frequently see being driven around. It appears to carry two huge gun barrels and something resembling the radiator of a butcher's refrigerator.

What and why is this? The need for this trailer was first appreciated when Crewe realised that putting power units on dynamometer tests is all very well, but test rigs are needed to check the overall performance of the car. Suppose, for instance, a giant hand could grip a car being driven on the road? Not only might it be possible to measure power output, and check efficiency of the whole transmission system, but the efficiency and reliability of everything from the engine to the tyre treads could be checked. This ideal requirement of a mobile test-bed induced the Motor Car Division to do rather better than the usual test, which with many other manufacturers consists simply of towing another vehicle around, and applying the brakes. A trailer vehicle was designed capable of absorbing up to 100 hp at 30 mph, remotely controlled from the towing car, and when necessary capable of keeping the overall speed constant irrespective of power input and road conditions or gradient.

This trailer weighs only 30 cwt, and carries an array of electric motors; the two resembling gun barrels are in fact 45-hp 3-phase induction motors rewired as DC machines, and up to 80 amps can be fed to the rotors. When the trailer is being pulled at 40 mph, the main rotor speed is 2,110 rpm, and this pull (controllable from the driving seat of the car) is enough to slow a Rolls-Royce down to about 12 mph. The ridged array looking like a refrigerator unit is the set of cooling fins on the dropping resistances for the control circuitry.

The trailer has saved probably around £250,000 in tests but, typical of Crewe's economy, is built up from the tail-end of a very old Rolls-Royce chassis with its rear-axle, now locked.

Four

SILVER WRAITH

G ENERALLY looked upon as the first post-war car from Crewe, the Silver Wraith was largely planned at Derby before the Second World War. It first came on the home market in 1947, and was in production until 1959, after the Silver Cloud was already established.

As the engineering student now knows, the power unit of the Silver Wraith stems directly from, and uses the same cylinder centres as, the original 20 hp six-cylinder engine designed by Sir Henry Royce in 1919. The Armed Forces had been supplied with well over 30,000 of these units during the four and a half years of war, and in common with most military equipment the engines were manufactured by techniques of quantity production alien to the hand-built philosophies of the Company in pre-war years.

As a Ministry of Aircraft Production official, I had discussions with Mr. W. A. Robotham in Derby, when he was chief engineer of the Motor Car Division, and he revealed a number of aspects of R.-R. thinking which led to the Silver Wraith.

'Our future policy is quite simple: to make the best motor-cars we can sell,' he said. 'This is perhaps not so simple as it sounds: we might make the best motor-car and not be able to sell it.

'The desire to make the perfect vehicle has to be tempered with the economic aspect of the matter. But there is no let-down whatever on quality. We still have the same rigorous qualifying test for any new component, which is that it has to run 20,000 miles on the road (or the equivalent) before it can be included in the production line. It still takes five years to get a car into production from the time we start designing it. But in 1939 we had begun to design a new range of cars. We had about 10 of these cars made before the outbreak, and finished two or three of them in the first month of war. We have had the exceptional experience of being able to run these cars for six years under ordinary conditions of everyday driving.

'In the progress of design we never make big jumps successfully. We have made them unsuccessfully, but these have never reached the public. The chief change from the pre-war to the post-war cars will be in making them simpler. The days have gone when all Rolls-Royce cars had a chauffeur. Royce really designed for the engineer. But today the owner-driver is largely predominant, and not perhaps five per cent of cars are chauffeur-driven. So we have gone in for simplification. We have also gone for increased durability. Our target for post-war cars is that they should be able to run 100,000 miles without a major overhaul, which on average means ten years. . . .'

Thus the Silver Wraith went into production at a swiftly changing time. As the world groped uncertainly for a more sure Peace than we had known in the '30's, there was now no need at Rolls-Royce for a production of 18,000 military aeroengines a year. Nearly 55,000 workpeople were no longer needed, and the bulk of 14,000 women and thousands more of semiskilled workmen punched their time-cards at Derby, Crewe and Glasgow for the last time, just as the first Silver Wraiths were being assembled. With overtime rates and war production bonuses, many women at Rolls-Royce had been earning £10 a week, equivalent then to the wages paid in Detroit today: but as the Company began to shrink to a peacetime norm, a nucleus of skilled craftsmen and technical staff were left to contrive the future. Glasgow, with the exception of a light-alloy factory, ceased for the time to exist as an R.-R. concern. Crewe went over entirely to the production of motor-cars, and the output of aeroengines was confined to the huge factory at Derby.

When the Silver Wraith was on the stocks, Sir Arthur Sidgreaves (knighted in the 1945 Honours List) was managing director of the Company. Continuing the R.-R. tradition of knowing everyone of note by an initial, Sir Arthur was just Sg to everyone. It was said that Sg was proud of having joined Napiers in 1902 at 'nothing a week', and began his real career in their salesroom shortly afterwards with a rise of 10s. He had, at the inception of the Silver Wraith, become one of the most approachable captains of industry (managing director at Derby since 1929), and a reporter once commented: 'It is no surprise to find a copy of the *Daily Herald* lying on his desk.'

Hs—E. W. (later Lord) Hives—was another of those who worked at the bench in the early days, and worked his way up, and I recall that when we talked together around the time I road-tested my first Silver Wraith, and when I enquired about the new policy, his reply was: 'Our policy has always been on an engineering basis. We are concerned all the time with producing the right article, for only if it is right can anyone do the selling.'

Joining Hs on the board in 1945 was E—A. G. Elliott—the Company's chief engineer, then, and a symbol of the continuity of design-policy from the days of Henry Royce. In that difficult period before the war when R's health had broken down and he was directing the development of design from his retreat on the Riviera, it was E, then a young designer working in daily contact with him, who transcribed his ideas into drawing-board statements for transmission to the experimental department at Derby. His presence in the team who ultimately produced the Silver Wraith ensured a consistency of design development since R died in 1933.

It would be interesting to know the present whereabouts of the very first Silver Wraith. It bore the series number 1SW1. For some time up to about 1947 it was used on experimental work, and later was sent to the Rolls-Royce driving school where in the hands of some 300 different drivers it clocked up a further 100,000 miles. Although Rolls-Royce Ltd. never disclosed bhp figures, the developed power on the Derby test-bed was just under 138 bhp; 125 in a chassis, and with the usual Rolls-Royce standard of silencing.

Contemporary description of the Silver Wraith put major emphasis on the power unit, 'It is an entirely new design', reported The Motor, 'having for the first time in Rolls-Royce history a combined cylinder block and crankcase, and an unusual form of valve gear, with the inlet valves placed in the head over the cylinder bores and the exhaust valves on the side of the cylinder block.' On 14th April, 1946, a complete technical survey of the new model was published in The Autocar, from which an abridged account of the general design philosophy is given here, and the comment was made that: 'This new valve arrangement is primarily dictated by the desire to obtain a short engine which at the same time affords adequate valve room, good breathing for the inlet valves, even cooling of valve seats, equal thickness of metal walls, good cooling of the sparking plug seats, and less complication of cores in the casting process.' Of the Silver Wraith as a whole, it was suggested that perhaps the particular charm of it: 'lies in the effectiveness with which all the undesirable manifestations incidental to the development of power by machinery have been skilfully exorcised. The result is a car which is a sentient being and is like a living thing.' A quarter of a century on, a succinct commentator would say: 'The Royce has been de-bugged.'

Rigidity was the keynote of the main-frame design, more than in any preceding 20, 25 or 25/30. Deep-section side members were braced together by a long, stiff cruciform central member, the ends of which were riveted and welded into the side members to form box sections. To provide a rigid base on which to mount the independent front suspension components, a large curved cross-member was provided across the front of the frame. Under this pan the i.f.s. layout had a type of suspension which was a further development of the pre-war Wraith design, in which a long link on each side is pivoted close to the centre of the front cross-member, and towards the rear is inclined to a joint at the bottom of the swivel pin yoke-piece. A second short link at the head of the yoke has its fulcrum in an hydraulic damper on the top of the frame. Then from the foot of the yoke a long strut runs backwards and inwards to a joint carried below the side member at a point close to the dash. On each side, of course, a stout coil spring is mounted between the lower link and the pin. By comparison with the earlier Wraith, the Silver Wraith has longer links and struts to enlarge the base of the triangulation, and this made it possible to have wider use of rubber bushes and so to obtain better insulation from road noise and shocks without introducing excessive flexibility. Rear suspension is by underslung half-elliptics, shot-blasted, with indented leaves, gaitered and fed from the central push-pedal oiling system. Pipes lead to the shackle-pins and spring leaves, with flexible pipes taking lubricant through the usual lettered and numbered drip plugs (different sizes for relative rates of oil emission) to the upper shackle-pins and leaves.

The steering mechanism is of the cam-and-roller Marles type as developed by Rolls-Royce. Track rods to the swivels are divided and jointed to a central lever linked back to the steering-gear drop-arm. For longevity, all the joints are spring-loaded on half-balls in phosphor-bronze bushes.

'The Best Car in the World' owes much not only to its Rolls-Royce heritage and designers, but to the craftsmen who build and test the cars. This view shows a small area of the Engine Testing Department at Crewe, in the mid-'50's, prior to the present electronic-controlled system of testing. Compare this modern photo with that on the facing page

Above Silver Wraith series engine on an exhibition stand, partly cut away to show construction. This series of power-units was first introduced in 1947 in 4,257-cc version, later increased (1951) to 4,566 cc, with automatic transmission, and (1955) to 4,887 cc
Below Vanden Plas Princess four-litre R engine produced by Rolls-Royce for The British Motor Corporation. This is a unit of 238·57 cu. in. (3,909 cc), 95·25 mm bore and 91·4 mm stroke, compression ratio 7·8:1

A modified Rolls-Royce mechanically driven servo motor (dry disc-brake type) is incorporated in a complex braking system in which front-brake operation is hydraulic and mechanical at the rear. Girling-type transverse expander wedges, adjusters and shoes are used back and front, but the front brakes are operated through Lockheed hydraulic equipment. Drive to the servo is from the gearbox which, of course, forms a unit with the engine, being supported on rubber mountings high at the front and at the rear below the tail of the gearbox; the reason for this layout is to obtain torsional flexibility and to minimise engine vibration being transmitted to the interior of the bodywork.

Similar vibration-free mounting is provided for the divided propeller-shaft. At the point where the division is made there is a central locating bearing, coupled to the frame by two links with rubber-bush bearings so that it is free to float in a lateral plane. The rear axle has hypoid bevel gears, and in place of the fully floating axle shafts which Sir Henry Royce used, semi-floating shafts were adopted, with flanges on the outer ends forged from the original bar to give a solid design of considerable strength.

As *The Autocar* pointed out, the evolution of the overhead-inlet, side-exhaust valve layout was part of the Rolls-Royce principle of developing with infinite care techniques which from long experience they find to give long-wearing life, refinement of running and enduring good power output. The o.i.s.e. arrangement avoids the complications of twin overhead camshafts, and also the restrictions in valve size incidental to overhead valves placed in line and situated in lozenge-shaped combustion chambers. The 'under and over' valve arrangement gives adequate space and allows large inlet valves to be used.

The exhausts are at the side of the block, operated by hollow, barrel-shaped tappets of chilled cast iron with relieved faces which bear down upon the specially profiled cams of a massive solid camshaft. This shaft in the early-series Silver Wraiths was driven through a two-to-one helical-toothed gear of fabric-reinforced plastic driven from a steel gear on the crankshaft. The rockers are hollow, and are pressure-fed from the drilled rocker shaft. The detachable cylinder head is of aluminium alloy, with valve seat inserts screwed in.

A dual downdraught aero-type Stromberg carburetter is used on the Silver Wraith, while twin SU's are fitted to the Mark VI

Bentley introduced at the same time. Heavily leaded fuels were still in use, following the wartime Pool petrol, so the Silver Wraiths and Mark VI's of 1946/7 had inlet and exhaust valves of special design, with a slight relief at the point where the stem issues from the guide. This was a device intended to break up formation of deposit from leaded fuel. Aerolite-type pistons with fluted skirts are used, with two gas rings and a slotted scraper, while the massive crankshaft and big-end bearings are of steel-backed Vandervell type with lead-bronze indium-faced linings.

On 8th October, 1963, Mr. S. H. Grylls, MA, who as chief engineer of the Motor Car Division played an important role in the continuing development of the Silver Wraith, delivered his classic paper 'The History of a Dimension' to the Automobile Division of the Institution of Mechanical Engineers. The title comes from one essential dimension which in the Rolls-Royce Company had not altered since 1919. This dimension is a centre distance of 4·15 in. between neighbouring cylinder bores of an in-line six-cylinder engine, and, as Mr. Grylls wryly commented: 'History will show that throughout 44 years of continuous development the gods have aligned themselves almost equally for us and against us.'

In *The Book of the Phantoms* I have already quoted freely from this paper, by permission of Mr. Grylls and of the Institution of Mechanical Engineers (he was then chairman of the Institution's Automobile Division), and in illustrating the development of the Silver Wraith's power unit I am again appreciative of permission to give the following information which applies especially to this model. Some abbreviation is necessary to emphasise that portion of the Rolls-Royce engine-development story relating to the Silver Wraith engine here under consideration.

'Immediately after the 1914–18 war,' says Mr. Grylls, 'Rolls-Royce recommenced manufacture of the Silver Ghost car but realised that a smaller model was required to meet the prevailing economic conditions . . . The first decision taken was to have a bore of 3 in. and a stroke of 4½ in. The Royal Automobile Club rating of this engine was about half that of the Silver Ghost—namely 20·6. From then on, the drawing-board settled the general layout, on these basic dimensions, of an engine known as I.G.-I. A cylinder bore centre distance of 4·15 in. was considered necessary to provide adequate intermediate bearings, and of

4·65 in. to provide a centre bearing. It was on the smaller of these two dimensions that the future development of the engine depended, and 4·15 in. proved an exceedingly good choice . . . The valve gear was of most advanced design, having two over-head camshafts. When I joined the Company 11 years later, the first engine was driving a chassis bump test rig, and one of my first jobs was to adjust the tappets. Far would it have been from me to criticise, but the job took a whole day. . . .

'The first engine was completed in 1920. Production of this smaller car was needed for the autumn of 1922. Its price had to be half of that of the Silver Ghost. Changes were made to the engine, and although a simpler push-rod version was chosen, most of the basic dimensions remained unaltered. . . . During the next 37 years, without increasing the cylinder centres, the output increased from 53 bhp at 3,000 rev/min to 215 bhp at 4,200 rev/min and eventually $3\frac{3}{4}$-in. diameter pistons had been squeezed into the same centre-distance. . . .

'The critical speed of the first production Rolls-Royce 20 hp engine was 3,300 rev/min, and equivalent to about 76 mph in top gear on the first series of cars. Luck was with us for a time. A little below this critical period the distributor ceased to function and the cam wheel came adrift. Even this happened very rarely as the flywheel at 3,100 rev/min had a resonance of its own, whose thunderous noise dissuaded most drivers from seeking an Elysium further on. Little was known in the early '20's about the necessary test-bed life of an engine, but it was thought that a car should be capable of 10,000 miles of full-throttle driving on straight French roads. In actual fact the white-metal bearings (direct in the case of the connecting rods) lasted for about 9,000 miles of this treatment. Until the advent of motorways, this engine had the reputation for lasting for ever on English roads.

'During the next seven years very few changes were made to the engine. . . . In 1930 the bore was increased to $3\frac{1}{4}$ in., there still being plenty of room for water between the bores. The critical speed had to be raised, a crankshaft with larger journals and crank-pins achieving 4,000 rev/min. . . . Throughout the years 1922–39 one problem never receded and, if anything, became more menacing. Between the inlet and exhaust valve of each cylinder was a narrow bridge of either iron or aluminium. As the ratio of valve diameter to bore size grew greater, so the bridge grew narrower; finally the foundry said that cooling of this bridge could no longer be guaranteed.

'Not wanting to tackle the noise of an overhead-camshaft engine, a decision was made in mid-1938 to design an engine with an overhead inlet valve and side exhaust. Such a configuration had already been designed, made and sold in very small numbers in 1903. It appeared again some twenty years later on the 3.9-litre Bentley, the last car made by the original company.[1]

'There was now no limit to the size of the inlet valve, only the mechanical difficulty of its operation. Remembering the smoothness of the iron engine experiment in 1932, the block and crankcase were made integral, the exhaust valve seating directly on to the iron surface. The gear compartment shrank to two gears, a steel crank pinion without spring drive, and a resin-bonded fabric cam wheel. Belts now drove the dynamo and water pump as well as the fan. The cylinder centres remained at 4·15 in., but the big-ends became narrower and the crank webs thicker to raise the critical speed of the crankshaft to 5,400 rev/min. . . . The war prevented any immediate sale of these engines, but an immense mileage was piled up in vehicles run as staff cars or converted to lorries. During the war the quality of plain bearings and poppet valves went forward enormously, all of which could be incorporated in the new iron engines. By 1946, French testing of cars had taken a new turn, at least 100,000 miles being required to make it necessary to look inside the engine.'

Eventually, as Mr. Grylls recounts, production began on the Rolls-Royce Silver Wraith and Bentley Mk. VI, both using a 3½-in. bore six-cylinder iron engine of 6·4:1 compression ratio.

[1] Mr. Grylls refers to the '4-litre' (3,915 cc) Bentley, which was basically a unit designed largely by Ricardo, fitted in a modified 8-litre Bentley chassis. Exhaust valves were slightly inclined to the vertical, the inlet valves being arranged in the detachable cast-iron head. Compression ratio was 5·5:1, the power output at 4,000 rev/min being 120 bhp. Combustion-chamber was of the Ricardo type. Mixture was by twin SU's. There was a seven-bearing crankshaft, and the push-rods for the inlet valves were, of course, concealed in the cylinder casting. The design owed little to W. O. Bentley, certainly not so far as the engine was concerned, and in his *Autobiography* (Hutchinson) he reminisced: 'The 4-litre was in effect a last desperate fling on which most of the firm's remaining resources were spent, but very few were sold because it wasn't a car that could be recognised as a Bentley at all. The Bentley clientele wouldn't have anything to do with push-rod engines. . . .'

The difference between the two engines now amounted only to camshaft and carburetter. A spring drive, similar to that of the pre-war engines, was added to deal with cam-gear rattles. The cylinder head was of aluminium to save weight, the camshaft was carburised, and exhaust valves again made of KE 965. At first the top 2½ in. of the cylinder bores were chromium-plated. Tappet adjustment had ceased to be a maintenance worry. The exhaust tappet adjustment low down on the side of the engine was far from accessible, but the clearance never varied.

'Engines proved exceptionally reliable,' recalls Mr. Grylls, 'although a few big-end failures, due to dirt which had not been caught in the bypass oil filter, pointed to the need for something even better. Nitrided shafts and lead-bronze bearings last for ever if fed with clean oil, but the combination is much less tolerant of dirt than the pre-war materials.

'In customers' hands the chromium part of the cylinder bore, about 0.0015 in. thick, lasted some 40,000 miles, after which bore wear shot up to 0.001 to 0.002 in. per 1,000 miles. Re-chromium plating a block was a costly business, the whole engine having to be dismantled, and all studs and gallery pipes removed from their casting.'

As detailed in Chapter One, the 1951 models were bored out to 3⅝ in. to give 4,566 cc, with compression ratio raised from 6·4 to 6·75. For 1955, boring out to 3¾ in. raised the capacity to 4,887 cc, and in 1957 the compression ratio was raised to 8:1. And although Rolls-Royce do not announce new models very frequently, a number of detail changes are incorporated as research and development shows the necessity. It is simple for the compiler of data to record engine numbers with relation to such changes, but in the engine development cells a good deal goes on which never reaches the final sales literature. A few of these troubles-which-never-get-to-the-customer have been related by Mr. Grylls. For example, the cylinder head proved remarkably resistant to a higher compression ratio achieved in the old way of machining metal off the face. A 7:1 compression ratio gave a little more torque, no more power, and a huge increase in roughness.

Eventually chromium-plating of the bores was abandoned, and instead a short pressed-in liner was used, of 30 per cent chromium content, 0·062 in. thick. Piston seizure on development tests continued for nearly two years, until a shape of skirt and crown ovality were found which combined quietness with reliability.

A force-feed of lubrication to the little-ends had been used by Rolls-Royce since 1919, and a gudgeon-pin diameter of 0·75 in. still sufficed. As an indication of R.-R. manufacturing accuracy, Mr. Grylls quotes an instruction from the so-called Rolls-Royce 'Bible' with regard to the fit of the gudgeon-pin in the yellow-metal bush of the connecting rod, to ensure quiet running: 'The fit must be such that the pin will not fall out under its own weight, but that the whole rod will just rotate under its own weight from a horizontal position.' In practice this meant a clearance of not more than 0·0002 in. nor less than 0·0001 in.

Continuing the story of the development of the engine used in the Silver Wraith, Mr. Grylls points out that the compression volume had become larger, giving more scope in the shaping of the combustion chamber, and a smoother engine appeared. 'It was then 1950. The first post-war cars were mounting in mileage, some having reached nearly 90,000 miles. Mysterious failures of cam-wheels started to occur, and always in France. Fabric had proved to have a finite life with rather a large scatter, the end being accelerated by higher-than-normal temperatures, always an adjunct of Routes Nationales.' (Various rigs were tried, and while development engineers preferred a soft material such as the original Fanroil wheel, aluminium was finally chosen because its cold failure strength could be quickly assessed, and it would not be subject to unpredictable time and temperature effects. Many Silver Wraith engines have been modified to take the aluminium-wheel camshaft drive, and the front casing is usually stamped with an 'A'.)

'Without any apparent effort,' comments Mr. Grylls, 'engines become more reliable the longer a basic design stays in use. Why not therefore increase the bore size a little further? . . . The introduction to the public of 3¾-in. bores (4·9 litres) coincided with an option to have automatic transmission.'

One reason for the immediate success of the Silver Wraith was its modern specification especially with regard to electrical accessories and instrumentation, even though the wheels were now only bolted-on pressed-steel discs, and what still appeared to be Rolls-Royce hub-caps were now stainless-steel pressings (shaped like a hub-cap) to keep the covering discs in place. Development was proceeding all the time and, as Mr. Grylls puts it: 'An organisation which makes entire engines does not make, design or develop many of the constituent or attendant pieces. It considers itself fortunate when extramural engineering keeps pace with internal requirement. The extramural engineering is shared by other engine makers, and only some outstanding and novel departure from the orthodox would leave it behind and find it wanting. Throughout the 40 years of this history, fuels, lubricants and metallurgy have kept pace with mep's and rev/min. This single sentence can be written because thousands of people have spent millions of pounds making it so.'

Five

DAWNS AND CLOUDS

'THE present Silver Dawn is in effect a remarkable example of what can be achieved by steady development engineering', commented *The Motor* in its road-test No. 16/54 of the Rolls-Royce Silver Dawn. 'In its original form the car which we were able to sample extensively in the Middle West of America did not seem to match up to the highest specification of road-holding and steering. Now, four years later, various modifications, coupled with a redesigned rear end, have transformed the handling qualities of the Silver Dawn.'

It is not generally realised that development of this nature did take place with the Dawn, which is sometimes dismissed as merely the export version of the Silver Wraith.

Of course, the Silver Wraith was available with left- or right-hand drive, and with the option (on LHD) of steering-column shift. From 1949 until 1953, however, the Silver Dawn certainly was an Export Only car, and most owners usually took the column change option. In 1952 automatic transmission was offered as an additional option, and by 1953 the Silver Dawn was also available for the United Kingdom market with automatic transmission standard as indeed it then was on the Silver Wraith. And, all the time, there was continuing development of chassis features, and of body styling. The Dawn has a 120-in. wheelbase, and no doubt many US owners regarded it as a luxury 'compact'. The standard four-door sports saloon retailed in the early 1950's at the oversea equivalent of £3,150, and of £4,195 for the Park Ward drop-head foursome coupé (convertible). At that same period, the price of the six-light Park Ward Silver Wraith saloon was £4,445 basic, or a UK total of £6,915 18s. 11d. including tax.

The Silver Dawn went out of production in 1955, on the introduction of the Silver Cloud, while, as we have seen, the Silver Wraith continued until 1958/9, at which time the Cloud series had become established, and (although the first-series

Cloud was not known contemporaneously as the 'Cloud I') the Cloud II was introduced.

The Motor's testers in 1954 said: 'One is left with a feeling that here is perhaps the finest owner-driver car yet to emerge from the distinguished factory.' When I tested one of the first automatic-transmission Dawn's, the basic price of £3,320 was inflated by UK purchase-tax to a total of £4,704 9s. 2d. (one wonders how many new Rolls-Royce Dawn purchasers actually did put that final 2d. on the cheque), and used-car prices prove that the Dawn is indeed a very good investment even though many of them have covered mileages well in excess of the magic 100,000.

In its day I found the automatic-transmission version did not give quite 16 mpg, and the top speed over a flying quarter-mile was 94 mph. However, the 18-gallon fuel tank seemed quite adequate for normal cruising, since at a steady 50 mph one could squeeze a consumption slightly better than 21 mpg, and with a 6·75:1 compression ratio (the first series was 6·4:1) the cheapest petrol would suffice. With a top-gear ratio of 3·73:1, open propeller shaft and typically quiet hypoid bevel final drive, the car simply glided, the engine just touching 1,000 rpm at 22½ mph.

By kicking down, one could move from standstill to 50 mph in rather better than 11 seconds. With the type of transmission adapted from the GM design and built entirely at Crewe, it is a simple matter to shift to position 3 on the selector, even when travelling at around 50 mph, to get a surge of power. If road conditions permit, the transmission then changes up again at about 60 mph. There is also an equivalent kick-down facility operated off the accelerator pedal. Exact change-up and change-down periods are controlled by the relay system, but when the accelerator is pressed fairly well down and the car is travelling on a level road, the change up to 2nd will take place at 30 mph, and to top at 57 mph. But a more gentle throttle application secures a quicker change, and the Dawn cruises easily at slow speed in top without unnecessary fussy gear-shifting.

As a quick getaway is important in traffic driving, I particularly noted an acceleration time of only 5 secs from standstill to 30 mph, and from a rolling start in about 4 secs. With a rather heavy brake-pedal pressure it was possible to get a crash stop of 33 ft at 30 mph, but the ordinary rolling stops needed a pedal pressure of barely 25 lb, giving the impression to newcomers to Rolls-Royce driving of a throttle-pedal feeling when braking.

Although the body-pressings were changed in certain details after the introduction of the Silver Wraith, the Silver Dawn was a 'standard steel saloon' like most of its Bentley counterparts. There were individual differences between the Dawn and the Mark VI. The Silver Dawn is the quieter car by far, while the Mark VI has more punch (partly because of the twin-SU carburation) and is slightly faster.

Some potential purchasers may eventually have plumped for the Bentley version, and there were rumours that having adopted an American-style automatic transmission system for the Silver Dawn (and from 1951 optionally for the Silver Wraith), the Company was proposing to introduce an American-style V8 power unit to satisfy the demands of the export market. Several experimental V8 engines were on the stocks, as we have seen, but wisely the Company finalised plans during 1953/4 to produce an entirely new body style before introducing a V8; and the policy decision was then also made to combine Rolls-Royce and Rolls-Bentley features entirely. For the first time since 1931, when the assets of Bentley Motors were acquired by Rolls-Royce,[1] the two cars became identical, apart from radiator shell, mascot and other insignia. With the introduction of the Cloud (in time to become known as the Cloud I) there was the companion Bentley S-type. After a long period of development, the Company had produced a composite version, a completely new chassis

---

[1] Bentley Motors, which won so many laurels for Britain in the triumphant 1930's, went into financial difficulties when one of its most distinguished Le Mans drivers—and, later, head of the company—millionaire Woolf 'The Babe' Barnato, was forced by his bankers to withdraw financial support. The Babe had driven Bentleys to gain 26 international class D records, and three times won the 24-Hours Grand Prix d'Endurance at Le Mans, but even a millionaire must obey his bankers when world depression threatens. Bentley Motors owed £40,000 to the London Life Association, and a receiver was appointed. Capt. W. O. Bentley hoped his company would be sold to Napiers, who would continue racing. However, Rolls-Royce outbid Napiers by just £1,000 and the Receiver agreed to R.-R. forming a new company, Bentley Motors (1931) Limited. For a time W. O. Bentley accepted a contract to work on engine design with Percy Northey, one of Royce's original team, but eventually left to design a V-12 unit for Lagonda. The first Derby-built Bentley, the 3,669 cc 3½-litre car, was based on the R.-R. 20/25. And until the advent of the Cloud there had always been essential design differences between Rolls-Royce and Rolls-Bentley cars.

frame and suspension, an engine of increased power, and a general grace and streamlining which put the whole design a decade ahead. The Bentley became the Rolls-Royce, and the Rolls-Royce became the Bentley, and neither lost in the transformation. Critics who aver 'It's no longer a Bentley' should recall that this was the first Rolls-Royce built since 1911 to be capable of a speed over 100 mph.

The Silver Cloud engine was, to Crewe, the logical development from previous Rolls-Royce and Bentley power units, with many modifications. An aluminium alloy cylinder head was used, with six separate inlet ports for easy breathing. A redesigned water-jacketed inlet manifold contributed to increased efficiency, while a revised exhaust system gave improved silencing with reduced back-pressure.

Even former-generation Bentley engine enthusiasts had to admit the Cloud is fine engineering. The nitrided crankshaft running in seven main bearings is something which only Crewe can produce. Aluminium pistons with three compression rings and one scraper, the top ring being chrome-plated: two diaphragm-type SU carburetters; full-flow high-pressure lubrication through an internal gallery to the main bearings and big-ends, and a low-pressure system lubricating the inlet rocker shaft, push-rods and tappets; this was now the outline of the engine behind either the Bentley or the 'square' radiator shell. The chassis is a closed box section of welded steel construction with cruciform centre-bracing pierced for the propeller shaft; steel front pan carrying the front suspension and steering, and box-section and tubular cross member at the rear. The centralised pressure lubrication system fed from a reservoir on the scuttle was retained for the Cloud. Suspension at the front is by wishbones of unequal length, with coil springs, and Rolls-Royce opposed-piston hydraulic dampers and torsional anti-roll bar. The rear suspension is by half-elliptic springs and Z type anti-roll bar, with electrically-controlled piston-type dampers. Diehards regretted the passing of the original graduated ride control. The Cloud's two-position switch on the steering column operates a solenoid working a control valve in the damper housing.

A Crewe designer at the time told me: 'To ensure consistent operation under the most severe conditions, no reliance is placed on any self-wrapping action between the shoes and the drums.

The front brakes have twin trailing shoes, these shoes being adjusted automatically so that clearance between shoe and drum is practically nil, and lost motion is eliminated. This means the speed of operation of the Rolls-Royce friction servo on the gearbox has been doubled. This servo motor applies the brakes through the hydraulic system which exercises a damping effect, ruling out the possibility of snatch or judder. The servo automatically proportions the braking effort between the front and rear wheels.'

Cast iron drums are used, with peripheral cooling fins, and for the Cloud the width of the drums was increased for the first time to 3-in. Wheel diameter was reduced from 16 in. to 15 in., carrying 8·20 broad-base tyres; these larger section tyres (the Silver Dawn was shod with 6·50 × 16) make for greater riding comfort and give longer tread life.

To the lay world, the greatest change between the Silver Wraith, the Dawn and the new Silver Cloud was the body styling—a design to be retained until the introduction of the Silver Shadow in 1965, and which remained fundamentally unchanged through the development of the Silver Cloud, the Cloud II and Cloud III. This styling was not only drawing-board stuff, but the result of extensive wind-tunnel tests in the Aero Division's test cells to get a body shape with low wind resistance, combined with a very low level of wind noise when travelling fast. Construction generally is in steel, to get maximum rigidity, but weight is saved by making the bonnet, doors and luggage locker lid in aluminium. A double-skin bulkhead on all cars in the three series of the Clouds provides an air-space between the power unit and the interior of the car.

A comprehensive heater and ventilation system was introduced. Heater and ventilation are independent, one at each side of the car, picking up fresh air through intakes above the front bumper (fender). Air is forced by the movement of the car, supplemented when needed by a ducted fan, through a heater matrix inside each front wheel-arch, and then passed into a transverse distribution box behind the instrument panel, from which it is fed to the screen and to the feet of driver and passengers. Each system is controlled by a knob on the instrument panel, with two push-pull positions and three positions of rotation. A separate duct outside the chassis frame ventilates the rear compartment. The distinguished motoring editor Thomas H. Wisdom when testing his first Silver Cloud commented: 'The push and pull controls on the dash board are of the violin type—the genuine Stradivarius touch.'

Of course conservative Rolls-Royce owners missed some features. The sunshine roof, for one. Obviating it was not an economy move, naturally, but the result of the Company's desire to get a safe, immensely strong body shell without appreciable wind noise. Provision of the fresh-air pumped ventilation system, with two $2\frac{1}{2}$-kW motors and a six-position control, made up for some of the features of a sunshine roof, and 'the Stradivarius touch', unlike the opening roof, did not produce a cold draught around the back of the neck. Strength and silence were the two immediate virtues of the Cloud body shell. One reason for the quiet ride is the almost complete insulation between body and chassis. As one critic noted: 'The only metal between the driving compartment and the chassis is the speedometer cable. . . . Unlike the average steel saloon, the doors close as they would on the old-fashioned coach-built body; and of course rattles do not come and go with changes of the weather.'

Tommy Wisdom gave the Cloud its first Press outing, took an S-type through the Alps and drove at Oulton Park, in the spring and summer of 1955. 'I can say from personal experience,' he said later, 'that in the Alps this big car can be handled uphill and downhill in perfect security. And it is the downhill test that is the sternest. Any average driver at the wheel of a good car can go quickly uphill. Downhill driving, particularly on a long and possibly treacherous Alpine Pass, with the average car great skill is required. But the new automatic gearbox, allied to the bigger, more powerful brakes, renders this example of "expert" driving child's play. The ability to lock the automatic gear system in second or third gears is the secret. Brake for a hairpin, accelerate, brake again, and so on—down the Stelvio my passengers did not realise that we went faster down this famous pass—Europe's second highest—than we went up, and that was very quickly! I was anxious to find out if the brakes faded in a long downhill run, for even some of the best cars have this failing. The brakes on the S-type were as good at Trafoi as they were at the summit—truly magnificent.

'What I and my passengers were intrigued by was the gentlemanly behaviour of the new car in the wet. My wife, who has raced, very quickly discovered that the car could be driven—the occasion was over secondary roads in the Alpes Maritimes—as fast in the wet as in the dry. We were really trying. We averaged from Grenoble to Turin 55 mph and all I can say is that a slightly nervous passenger, as most drivers are away from the wheel, sat comfortably and viewed the scenery! That was both impressive and unusual, my wife said. My next memorable impression of the new car—both models, in fact—was at Oulton Park motor-racing course in August. The Silver Cloud and the S-type were both on duty as Stewards' cars during an international race meeting. I took the opportunity of having a fast run round this interesting and twisting circuit and, quite unofficially, beat the 1954 lap record for saloon cars.'

The London *Daily Mail* gave one of the new cars as first prize in 'The Greatest Car Contest of All', and offered Stirling Moss the chance to test it.

'It was rather like sleeping on a feather-bed after roughing it on a park bench,' explained Moss afterwards. 'One day I was tearing round the Monza circuit in the 180 mph Vanwall, deafened by the roar of its 280 hp engine and wrestling it through the corners with arms that ached. The next, I was behind the wheel of a Silver Cloud, lounging in a luxury seat with the radio playing and wondering if there really was an engine under that noiseless bonnet. . . .'

He explained that he approached the task with a certain amount of prejudice, for this was a very different sort of car from the sort he then usually drove . . . 'and Rolls-Royce designers are notorious for the way they shy away from anything revolutionary or even advanced. At first I did not think the driving seat suited me very well even though the back-rest is adjustable, and I was a little surprised to find that there were no press-button controls for either the seat or the window. I missed the sunshine roof of my own saloon. But, my word! How this car grows on you. . . .

'It does not feel like a big car at all, and this is largely due to its excellent system of power-assisted steering. If you were buying the car, this feature would cost an extra £165, including tax, but it is so good that I was not surprised to learn from Rolls-Royce that nine out of every ten buyers of the Silver Cloud ask for powered steering . . . You get most benefit from this, of course, in town driving. I was afraid that out in the country I should miss the feel of the front wheels as I turned the steering—a point that is so important where safe driving is concerned. I need not have worried. The Rolls-Royce engineers have somehow managed to retain that vital quality. And apart from being delightfully light to control, the steering is agreeably self-centring. . . . Eighty miles an hour is for the Silver Cloud a gentle cruising speed, and the needle of that ever-so-accurate speedometer swings round to the 80 mark in well under half a minute from a standing start.' (*The Silver Dawn took 31 secs from standstill to 80 mph when I first tested it, but the tester of a motoring journal reduced this to 29.2 secs.—Ed.*) 'The acceleration is impressive, but with it all the car is as quiet and gentle as a lamb. Not only the engine. The wind noise has been kept down to a minimum. . . . The Silver Cloud has an automatic gearbox. It is fitted as standard, as, of course, it should be. For although I am a racing driver, and my bread and butter largely depends on the speed with which I change the gears on my Grand Prix cars, I want nothing of it when it comes to ordinary driving . . . I want my private motoring to be as easy and comfortable as I can get. I'm not much of a one for sports cars, really. . . . We all know that there's very little difference— apart from their radiators—between the S-series Bentley and the Rolls-Royce Silver Cloud. Yet those distinctive front grilles seem to give the two models completely different characters, and you can understand anyone being willing to pay £150 extra, in-cluding tax, for the completely forgivable snobbery of driving behind that classic Rolls radiator. Now I know why the Queen uses her Rolls for so much of her motoring. Now I know why Rolls-Royce cars are used by such famous people as General Franco, the Shah of Iran, the Ruler of Kuwait, Grace Kelly . . .'

Although the official Rolls-Royce Handbook on the Silver Cloud carries the time-honoured heading 'The Secret of Suc-cessful Running,' and starts 'An owner would do well to instruct his driver as follows . . .' the Cloud was recognised to be very much an owner-driver's car. The Hythe Road School of Instruc-tion was open to 'owner-drivers and/or members of their families', and not only to chauffeurs. And despite continuing argument as to whether the Rolls-Royce had become Bentleyised, or vice versa, the quality and the guarantee remained just as in the early days of the Company.

'This chassis of the Rolls-Royce Silver Cloud (and Bentley S-series) is guaranteed for a period of three years,' each new owner was told. And: 'Motor cars are inspected at owners' residence in Great Britain throughout the period of the Guaran-tee, to ensure that they afford the utmost satisfaction in service.'

Six

ENGINE DEVELOPMENT

IT used to be held that Rolls-Royce Motor Car Division designers were hide-bound, conservative and too security-minded. They did not even allow engine brake horsepower figures to be disclosed.

This secrecy, if it existed, was certainly broken down by Mr. S. H. Grylls who gave his now-classic Paper 'the History of a Dimension' to the Automobile Division of the Institution of Mechanical Engineers on 8th October, 1963; as we have seen in Chapter Four, this made frank, informative disclosures of the Company's design philosophy, and of problems overcome through the years, with the growth of the 20 hp model of 1922 through a period of the next 37 years, to the Silver Wraith. But this Paper is concerned with the 'Dimension', cylinder centres of 4·15 in., and with the whole series of in-line engines, and the Paper must be read carefully to see that development of the V8 was already in progress.

In a witty feature for *The Times British Motoring Survey* in October, 1965, entitled 'Sybaritic Ladies of the Road' ('Sybarite, inhabitants of ancient Greek colony of Sybaris in Italy, noted for luxury,' says the Oxford Dictionary), a title which links the present series of Silver Shadows with the sybaritic female Spirit of Ecstasy, Mr. Grylls said: 'Engineering departments have to think well ahead; the aluminium V8 engine was, for example, first planned in 1947. . . .'

. Dr. Llewellyn Smith once told me that the Motor Car Division needed to freeze styling ten years ahead, and part of their job was to sense public taste 12½ years ahead, to allow for getting into production. ('Twelve and a half years is a long time even for Rolls-Royce. That is why we cannot be lumbered with design gimmicks.') But the ordinary businessman may well wonder why, if a V8 engine was running at Crewe back in 1947, it was not in production until 1958.

Explains Mr. Grylls, to the Institution of Mechanical Engin-

Above Crankcase bottom face of the 90° V-8 power-unit, showing support buttresses. Ultimate smoothness of the engine depends to a considerable extent upon structural stiffness of the crankcase. High beam stiffness has been achieved in horizontal and vertical planes, and for an 8-cylinder unit the crankcase is deep, short and rigid

Below Under-bonnet view of the Silver Shadow, the series introduced in 1965. This view shows the twin SU carburetters, air trunking, hydraulic reservoirs, and belt-driven refrigerant pump

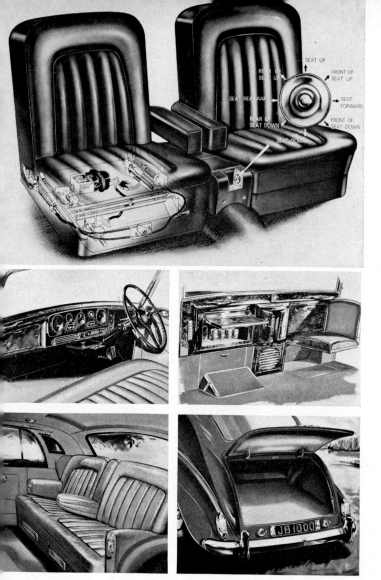

Above Front-seat layout and controls on the Silver Shadow. To adjust the seat, the switch control knob is moved to the desired direction (e.g. control moved to '3 o'clock position' for 'Front of seat up') of ultimate seat movement. Back of each seat is manually adjusted for rake

Below Luxury fittings in a Phantom V. These pages from the James Young catalogue depict *(top left)* the figured walnut instrument panel incorporating demister and heater controls, and passenger's table, *(top right)* back of the division incorporating extra seats, footrests and cocktail cabinet, *(bottom left)* rear compartment with centre arm-rest and reading lights, and *(bottom right)* carpet-lined luggage boot

eers: 'In 1947, with a view to a long-term future, an eight-cylinder "B-range" engine was cast in aluminium and was equipped with dry liners. . . . With three carburetters this engine ran for some years in a long-nosed Bentley, giving considerable enjoyment to the driver but never seeing the production light of day.

'The War Office, hearing of this car, ordered for test some six-cylinder B60 engines of similar construction. This project was dropped, except that one of the engines found its way into an experimental car. About 1952 a chance remark in America suggested that these aluminium engines would work just as well if the dry liners were removed. An old War Office engine was extracted from store, the liners were removed and 3⅝in. pistons were fitted at their usual running clearance. This engine survived a test-bed gruelling and a year or so in a car then, like its predecessors, was forgotten. . . .'

It should be explained that the B-range of engines, from which the first experimental V8 was formed, had as its original conception the object of providing a series of compact petrol engines having a common bore and stroke, and covering a power range up to 235 hp. They are made in three basic sizes, four, six and eight cylinders, and up to 1958, when the car V8 engine was well established and ready for the production line, more than 20,000 of the B-range engines had been produced. Typical applications of the B-range included the B-40 (four-cylinder) unit in the Austin Champ, in the Dennis ambulance, and the hydraulic power unit for the Centurion bridgelayer tank; the B60 and B61 (six-cylinder units) in the Humber 1-ton '4×4' military truck, Dennis fire appliances, Daimler Ferret Scout car, rotary snow ploughs, and a 14-ton motorway gritter/snow-plough. The B80 (eight-cylinder) unit was introduced for the Mk. VII harbour tug and the Thorneycroft fire crash tender, Nubian crash tender, Alvis Saracen armoured personnel carrier, and the Saladin armoured car. The B81 is in Leyland tractors, RAF and RCAF fire crash tenders, and many big vehicles including the Hispano-Suiza HS. 30 tracked carrier. Of course it would distress admirers of veteran and vintage vehicles to think the day would come when an Hispano would be found with a Rolls-Royce engine: but progress is inevitable!

Initially the B-range consisted only of the B40, B60 and B80, having four, six and eight cylinders respectively. They were designed to give maximum interchangeability between components, and covered a power range of between 80 and 175 bhp gross. By increasing bore size from 3·5 to 3·75 in. dia., raising the compression ratio and improving manifolding and breathing, it became possible to extend the range to 235 bhp gross. In the intermediate range the power of the six-cylinder engine was increased from 130 to 168 bhp. In addition to the wearing parts, of which almost 90 per cent are common throughout the B-range, the interchangeability of such items as wheelcases, clutch housings and coolant pumps makes possible by 'cannibalisation' the rapid repair of engines under all conditions. A subsequent series, the K-range, was subsequently developed for military and commercial markets, and the salient feature of the K-range is the facility for multi-fuel operation; they work on petrol, diesel oil or aviation kerosene, and are interchangeable with the B-range.

Now while 1947 had seen an experimental B 80 eight-cylinder engine driving a long-nosed Bentley on secret test runs around the British Isles, what of the V8's progress? The answer was given by Mr. A. J. Phillips, whose Paper 'The Design History of a V8 Engine' was delivered to the Automobile Division of the Institution of Mechanical Engineers. This Paper has been referred to in Chapter Three, and was in fact received at the IME in December, 1961 (followed by a meeting of the Automobile Division in March, 1962), which was all a considerable time prior to Mr. Grylls' outline of the history of that Dimension. Thus it will be seen from 1961 until 1963/4 the Company made a very full and detailed disclosure to the engineering world of what went into the development and testing of the whole range of in-line four, six and eight-cylinder units, and also the V8; so one may wonder if that criticism is not ill-founded that Rolls-Royce is too security-minded.

But still, a critic may aver: 'Despite all this, it is hard to ascertain the exact bhp figures, to know how the present-day Rolls-Royce V8 compares, for example, with those built in Detroit. What performance does it really give? And how will it stand up to a bashing?'

The answer is given in Mr. Phillips' Paper: 'This engine, with all essential auxiliaries including bell-housing and exhaust manifolds, achieves a figure of 2·7 lb/hp coupled with an endurance capability of more than 400 hours' full throttle at 4,200 rev/min without any failure.'

This outstanding result became possible when Crewe's design

team set out to produce a successor to the 4·9 litre in-line six-cylinder engine which, at the time, had some 20 years of development behind it. The power potential was to be at least 50 per cent greater than the in-line six, there was to be no increase in weight, as little increase in cost as possible, a level of silence, smoothness and reliability at least as high as that previously achieved, and finally it was essential the engine should fit into the same bonnet space as that occupied by the in-line six. A V-form of engine was almost inevitable.

Says Mr. Phillips: 'The project was therefore an "all-aluminium" wet-linered V8 of approximately 3·8-in. bore, 3·5-in. stroke (giving 5·2 litres but having cylinder spacing large enough to allow an increase in swept volume of up to 6 litres), 7·25:1 compression ratio; the short stroke being dictated as much by bonnet side clearances as the more technical reason of increased crankshaft rigidity.' It will be appreciated there has been continuing development of Crewe's V8 engine since the team began. The 6¼-litre engine was introduced for the Silver Cloud II and Phantom V; and in the current Silver Shadow there is a new cylinder head design giving better breathing, and bringing the spark plugs above the exhaust manifold. It used to be said of the early series that 'one has to change a front wheel to change the plugs'.

The following technical survey of the development of the Rolls-Royce V8 engine, by permission of Rolls-Royce Ltd. and of the Institution of Mechanical Engineers, is an edited, abbreviated version of Mr. A. J. Phillips' Paper, together with the Communications and subsequent IME discussions in London, Derby and Warrington. From these discussions it may be observed, before dealing with the modern engine development, that of course Royce himself made many improvements in the field of V8 engines, and his Patent No. 23,557 of 18th January, 1906, covered V8 layout and gear drives for oil and water pumps. This layout included a number of features (tappet lever between cam and tappet, vertical valves, and gear-type oil pump, for example) which were in due course incorporated into the Silver Ghost. The flat cranks of the nickel-steel forged crankshaft had the throws set at 180-deg., and the whole engine was reasonably compact. Naturally there were other V8 pioneers in those days, too. At an IME discussion it transpired that a company later to become world-famed, ENV, was formed in 1910 to build aero

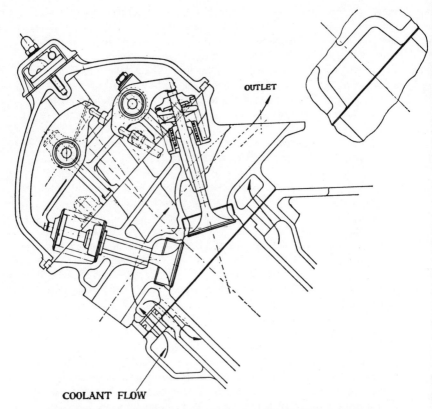

OUTLET

COOLANT FLOW

Cross-sectional drawing of the experimental 'wide' cylinder
head, showing coolant circulation

engines of a French V8 design. This was known as *'le moteur en-V'*,
hence the company adopted the name ENV Motors. It was an
ENV 60 hp engine powering the Howard-Wright biplane in
which T. O. M. Sopwith made the first flight across the English
Channel by an all-British aircraft in December, 1910, six months
after the Hon. Charles Rolls' untimely death in another Wright
biplane.

Two basic engines were produced during the first experimental
period, these being the wide and narrow respectively, with different valve layout. It was planned to use a two-plane crank-

shaft, with 90-deg. banks, so even firing intervals could be achieved. Inlet manifolding is made difficult by uneven firing on each individual bank of cylinders. A single-plane (normal four-cylinder) crankshaft gives even firing on each bank and is easier for carburation, but involves large secondary vibrations which Crewe's designers could not accept.

As for all-aluminium construction, this alloy has the propensity ('nay, eagerness,' says Mr. Phillips) to transmit noise freely. This, coupled with a low modulus of elasticity and high notch sensitivity, makes it a difficult material to use for a crankcase. Tests on the beam stiffness of the crankcase during development proved it to be much less flexibile than the cast-iron in-line six engine. And to suggestions the V8 crankcase could be built up in steel, or on other ways, Mr. Phillips said: 'Even Rolls-Royce cannot afford the luxury of fabricated construction for an automotive crankcase; in any case I would think thin steel will transmit noise even more effectively than aluminium.'

A fully heat-treated 4 per cent silicon-aluminium alloy, LM8, is the material used for the cylinder block casting (he says), and in this condition a minimum Brinell hardness of 80 and an ultimate tensile strength of 15 to 17 tons to the square inch is attained. Although reputedly it has only fair machining qualities, its casting fluidity and good corrosion resistance make it one of the better light alloys for this purpose. The cylinder liners, produced from centrifugally-cast high-phosphorous iron pots, are sealed by direct contact between the underside of the top flange and the cylinder-block counter bore, the 'nip' being controlled to approximately 0·002 in. Separate coolant and oil seals at the skirt end of the liner are provided by rubber rings located in grooves machined into the cylinder block. Tell-tale drillings between the grooves were initially made to indicate any leakage of oil or coolant past these rings, but during the whole series of initial tests of this engine not one case of leakage occurred. The bores were honed to a finish of approximately 30 micro-inches to provide an oil-retaining surface, and the outer diameters of the liners were given a protective coating of lacquer on the surface exposed to coolant.

There is far more in the design of a cylinder block for such an engine than the layman may suppose. For example, a number of now historic Phantom III's have suffered from corrosion, and complete elimination of corrosion is almost impossible to achieve.

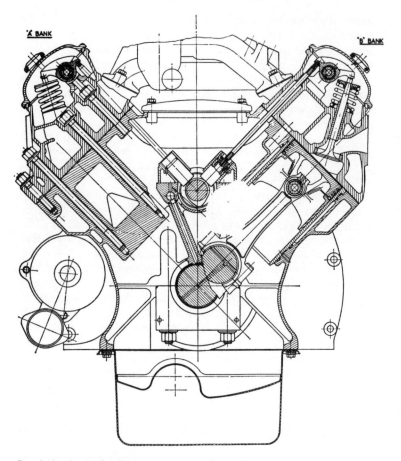

Section through the experimental 'narrow' engine from which the final V–8 unit was developed for the Silver Cloud and Phantoms V and VI

In the present V8 an effort has been made to reduce the rate of coolant flow through the cylinder block and increase the pressure, whilst maintaining a high rate of flow through the heads. Mr. Phillips has explained that high flow rates around cylinder liners could give rise to dangerously low pressures, which in turn could induce the onset of cavitation erosion. The coolant system of the Silver Shadow is pressurised, and it is the policy to use 85-deg.C. thermostats which are beneficial to good car heating and high running temperatures.

A feature of the first V8 cylinder head was the very short exhaust elbows (later modified), and a good deal of time was spent reducing the area of coolant over these ports to avoid the necessity for a larger radiator than that used to cool the smaller 4·9-litre six-cylinder engine. In fact the heat-to-coolant was reduced from 76 per cent of the power output in the case of the six to only 54 per cent in the V8.

Contrary to contemporary Detroit practice, the gear-driven camshaft is carried in four bearings and rotated in a trough formed as an integral part of the crankcase. The more usual arrangement is to provide five bearings and to allow the camshaft to be exposed to crankcase oil-splash. The main design reasons were that reducing the length devoted to bearings gives more room for cams and tappets, and an oil-bath rather than crankcase splash can ensure better low-speed lubrication of tappets.

The first series Phantom III's had hydraulic tappets, to provide a quiet means of valve opening. The principle is that of an hydraulic buffer as part of the cam-follower, and the system should be self-adjusting. These were satisfactory when Phantom III's were new, but as the years rolled on and the internals of the engine became sludgy, operation of the hydraulic tappets was unreliable; many Phantom III's have now been converted to solid tappets—a task which in the 1930's cost almost as much as a baby car! The Jowett Javelin (horizontally-opposed flat-four engine) used hydraulic tappets, but generally the design is far too costly because of the gun-like precision needed to produce them. Even among Detroit cars, General Motors confined them chiefly to Cadillac and Buick.

It is of interest that experimental V8 engines for the Phantom V were tried out with solid tappets, but in an all aluminium engine they were found noisy at times, the reason being that the differential expansion condition, with hot coolant and cold oil, could account for an increase of 0·02 in. valve-train clearance. This made a 'lash adjuster' or hydraulic tappet essential to achieve a Rolls-Royce standard of silence and first experiments used one designed by Chrysler's. Inlet valves of the first prototype V8 had a head diameter of 1·75 in., and the Stellite-faced and tipped exhaust valves 1·5 in. The same cam form was used for each, giving a lift of 0·345 in. Inlet valve guides were of cast iron, and to avoid scuffing troubles the exhaust guides are of phosphor-bronze. Of course the V8 was designed right from the start for an associated automatic transmission system, and it is interesting that in the design stage a small valve overlap was chosen to reduce tick-over speed to a minimum, and of course this also reduces the tendency to creep, on a hydraulic coupling.

In Chapter Three we saw what care is devoted to fabrication of the crankshaft, which is forged from EN 19, then heat-treated. Five copper-lead main bearings are provided. Aluminium-tin bearings have been used experimentally at Crewe, but the present preference is for copper-lead bearings with an overlay. As we have seen, no special locking device is used on con-rods nuts, and at an IME discussion in Warrington, Mr. Phillips explained: 'If a connecting rod is tightened up properly and the faces are nicely made, this is the best lock one can obtain. Of course if it is not tightened up properly it will fail in fatigue, which will soon become obvious, and no locking device will prevent failure. At a similar discussion in Derby, a member of the Aston-Martin team admitted they had experienced some trouble initially owing to loss of oil due to increases in clearance of the main bearings as the engine warmed up. Mr. Phillips replied that, by comparison, the Rolls-Royce V8 did not rotate so quickly, but the main factor is that the bearing clearances are quite small ($2\frac{1}{2}$ thou at room temperature) and there has been no trouble at all through loss of oil in production engines. 'During development of the engine we had reports of slight rumblings from the bottom end,' but they do not happen now.

Oil consumption of the V8 is good, at least 4,000 mpg being obtained, and it is recommended the sump be drained at 6,000-mile intervals.

Twin SU HD.8 carburetters are used on the present production engine, and a number of questions have been asked by visitors to Crewe as to the apparent complex induction system, and why Rolls-Royce do not favour fuel-injection. Says Mr. Phillips: 'It is not generally realised how much greater are the air movements in a two-plane V8 engine than an in-line six unit, where both centre cylinders reciprocate in unison rather than in opposition. . . . The induction tract is coupled to the two banks of cylinders by faces as near horizontal as conveniently possible, to avoid the effect of differential expansion. Blocks run at a higher average temperature that that achieved by manifolds. . . . Several initial designs made use of dual downdraught carburetters of American origin, mounted on a conventional two-duct manifold system and having the minimum of duct-heated area. . . . But the distribution was unsatisfactory, and a second type was designed having sharp corners between the risers and branches, and a greater degree of tract heating. Now all induction tracts have a cross-sectional area of 2·5 sq. in. The usual Rolls-Royce automatic choke system is employed, with one major difference; the previous water-heated bi-metallic coil-operated choke butterfly valve is now operated through the medium of hot air drawn through a 'choke stove' situated in the near-side exhaust manifold.

'The major problem has been overcome, which was that of modifying the system to fit neatly into the V with opposing carburetters, rather than the side-by-side arrangement of the in-line engine. The consequent increase in the number of bends in this system, coupled with an increased length of tract in the air side, gives rise to a greater loss of head . . . but the areas are kept as generous as possible, and torque is not unduly repressed.' (At an IME discussion, a leading engineer, formerly a Rolls-Royce apprentice at Derby in the middle 1930's, made the jocular comment that they should discard the present manifold system and fit eight motorcycle-type carburetters! 'Your final design of induction pipe is a masterpiece,' he told his former colleague Mr. Phillips. 'It should guarantee that the mixture is so dizzy by the time it reaches the inlet ports that it doesn't really know if it is trying to go in or come out!)

As to the frank questions about fuel-injection, at various times Mr. Phillips has dealt with this, the gist of the information being: 'We have thought of fuel injection, and dismissed it. . . . It is very much cheaper and better to use carburetters for this job. With good manifolding, what is to be gained by fuel injection? Surely only the pressure-drop across the choke? . . . The carburetter provides a satisfactory air/fuel ratio throughout the running range, although of course this can be destroyed by bad manifolding. The V8 induction system may look wrong aerodynamically, but it does provide reasonably good distribution. . . . More could be lost by poor distribution than is gained by good aerodynamic efficiency. . . . Although fuel injection is a wonderful way of overcoming distribution problems, there is the difficulty of cost: probably ten times the cost of a carburetted system. . . . The better a carburetted induction system, the less need there is to resort to fuel injection; moreover, there is very little to be gained by its use.'

Much of Crewe's initial V8 research was done on the first of the two basic designs described, the 'wide' one with a centrally-placed spark plug, and the 'narrow.' It was a modified form of the narrow engine which finally went into production, and as a result of a demand for a considerable increase in torque, the swept volume was increased to 6·23 litres by boring out from 3·8 to 4·1 in., and increasing the stroke from 3·5 to 3·6 in. The cylinder head in the first of this series employed a ramp-type combustion chamber having a high squish ratio of 33 per cent (the earlier central-spark-plug engine with the different valve layout had a ratio of 20 per cent), and this reduced the ignition advance to approximately half that necessary with the wide engine.

As Mr. Phillips sums up: 'No reduction in specific power resulted from the use of in-line valves, and the engine was slightly less "carbon conscious" than its predecessor. The use of a single rocker shaft and shorter valves operated by lighter rockers in a more compact head, together with other significant weight reduction measures, brought the overall weight below the previous 4·9-litre in-line engine by almost 30 lb., and enabled the target of "no increase in weight" to be achieved.'

And so the V8 was announced in 1958, and was used for the Silver Cloud II, and the Phantom V. But what of the classic in-line six? Production continued in the B-range and multi-fuel K-range, but from 1958 to 1961 a number of other policies were being considered, and at length in December, 1961, came the announcement from Crewe: 'The British Motor Corporation Ltd. and Rolls-Royce Ltd. are examining the feasibility of technical collaboration between them in the field of motor car engineering. . . . It seems there must be a fund of knowledge at both of the companies which could be used to mutual advantage. What we are proposing to do is to start discussions in depth among our engineers. . . .' There was no further announcement until July, 1964, when the first result of the cooperation was seen between R.-R. and BMC, the Vanden Plas 4-litre Princess R, with a 175 bhp six-cylinder engine, the FB60.

I was at Longbridge that July when the wraps were taken off

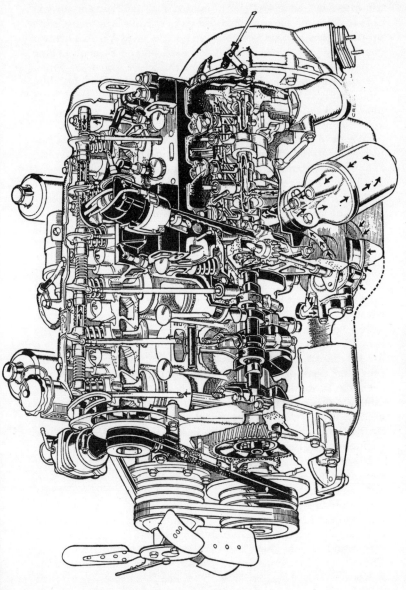

Cut away diagram of the 4-litre R engine (3,909 c.c.) somewhat similar to that used in the Silver Wraith series, produced for the Vanden Plas Princess saloon

the first Royce-engined ('R') Vanden Plas saloons, and so was able to discount rumours that 'this is how Rolls-Royce are using up their stock of sixes now they've gone over to V8's'. This was completely untrue, for the FB60, based on the B-range engine rather than any in the Silver Wraith, Silver Dawn or Silver Cloud, was specially tailored for the Princess. Dr. Llewellyn Smith and Sir George Harriman told me production had been planned on the basis of a maximum of 12,000 cars a year and involved considerable capital investment at Crewe and Derby.

'We have installed a considerable amount of new and completely up-to-date plant for this job,' said Dr. Llewellyn Smith, 'The firm of Vanden Plas is very well known to Rolls-Royce. I should think that up to the Second World War they made more bodies for R.-R. and Bentley chassis than for any other make.'

On the road the Princess R was distinguished by being 12 mph faster than the C-series, reaching 50 mph in three-quarters of the time from standstill, and using only some 2 mpg more for much greater power output. As we have already seen, the in-line six car engine was stretched to 4·5 litres in 1939 (for the Wraith) and further enlarged to 4·9 litres in 1954 in conjunction with an inlet-over-exhaust valve gear layout, which was then incorporated in 1947 and used on all Rolls-Royce and Bentley cars for the next seven years. Largely because of military demand for the B-range version, the capacity was reduced from 4·9 to 3·9 litres by shortening the stroke from 111·4 mm to 91·44 mm. This raised the peak of the power curve from 4,500 to 4,800 rpm. At the same time, the weight was reduced from 625 to 450 lb. by using an all-aluminium block (an alloy head was already being used), with inserted dry liners, and pressed-in valve seats. At this figure, the Crewe engine is 85 lb. lighter than the BMC 2·9-litre engine used in the other Vanden Plas models.

It is a common criticism of the all-aluminium engine that, by reason of the high thermal expansion, stiffness is reduced and also noise is increased. However, the Crewe designers overcame these difficulties ingeniously. Automatic tappets were used for inlet and exhaust valves. These give controlled clearances almost immediately after the engine starts. A design of piston was incorporated which gives low clearance within the iron liners. These liners, incidentally, are pressed into the alloy block after it has been oven-heated. Finally, there is a closely-controlled 'nip' on the main-bearing caps (these are also of aluminium), the retaining set-bolts being waisted, and the nuts tightened to a precise degree of torque so they are stretched to the elastic range and are therefore self-locking. The whole of the block was anodised to prevent corrosion.

Among the many ingenious features of the FB60 is the design of the exhaust valves. They are made of KE 965, which has exceptional fatigue resistance, and the valve face and tip are both treated with Stellite (as in the V8), which of course is a cobalt-base alloy having immensely strong resistance to wear. Top faces of the valves are coated with Valray, which is a nickel-chrome material having a marked antipathy for carbon, and this reduces any tendency in an all-alumimium engine for carbon to result in detonation and undue noise. Another detail of this FB60 design is that the exhaust valve springs face against flexible washers, deflection of which gives a slight angular motion each time a valve opens. The cylinder head used is of a type giving controlled combustion, so the relatively high BMEP of 138 psi is attained without use of high-octane fuel.

In this form, the FB60 was used in the Princess R from September, 1964 onwards, in conjunction with the Borg Warner Model 8 automatic transmission. It was the first BMC car of its type to have a top speed of around 110 mph, and the Princess R sold for a basic price of £1,650 (plus tax). The type of Borg Warner transmission chosen was then new to Britain. It is essentially different from the GM system now used in the Silver Shadow, but it incorporates a fluid torque converter in conjunction with a three-speed hydraulically-operated planetary gearbox.

It was noted by income-tax accountants and others that although the Princess R used a Rolls-Royce engine, had power-steering, and a pleasant body-shell having at least some points in common with that now designed for the Silver Shadow, the two cars met a totally different market: and it was also noted that out of the (then) all-up United Kingdom cost of a Silver Cloud II of £5,802 7s. 6d., just over £1,707 was purchase-tax, £50 more than the basic cost of a complete Princess R!

This philosophy of a quality car with a Rolls-Royce engine, on the market at a shade under £2,000, satisfied many people, and no doubt in particular Mr. S. B. Bailey, MSc, MIMechE, himself a former Rolls-Royce man, who during a technical discussion on the V8 design commented: 'For many years between the

1914–18 and 1939–45 wars Rolls-Royce have made available two different engine sizes—the 3½-litre for the fastidious motorist who likes to be able to get 16-20 mpg, and the 7-litre for the millionaire who didn't even know the car used petrol. The millionaire has been almost entirely replaced by the expense-account tycoon, but public opinion is moving against him, and the government has already limited him to a £2,000 motor-car. This is one of the clumsiest pieces of legislation which has ever been enacted. . . .'

Seven

GATHERING CLOUDS

M OTOR Shows are mad events, where on almost every
exhibition stand but one people fling open doors and
bonnets and boot lids, scramble in and out of driving compart-
ments, and sit silently at the steering-wheel, planning, dreaming,
hoping.

The one exception had always been the Rolls-Royce stand,
where tradition had it that all car doors were locked, for pretty
obvious reasons. In time the Rolls-Royce stand became little
more informative than a mere coachwork exhibition, since
nobody could twiddle the controls, let alone see anything so
inelegant as an engine. Then came the London International
Motor Show of 1959. For the first time an engine was on show.
And no wonder, for it was of course the 6¼-litre all-aluminium
V8 unit the development of which we have followed in the preceding chapter, and which now was available for the Silver
Cloud II (at first they called it the 'S.2' engine) and the new
Phantom V. So a polished exhibition-stand version of the V8
was on show, and even the Company unbent sufficiently to
describe it as a landmark.

'Before the S-series of cars was announced in 1955,' they said,
'it was realised that a larger engine would be needed to give
swifter acceleration. Work started on an eight-cylinder design.
The obvious choice would have been a straight-eight engine
which Rolls-Royce have been producing for thirteen years for
use in military vehicles. But the length of this unit would have
created undesirable characteristics, and the shorter, stiffer over-
square V8 layout was decided upon. The R.-R. design team had
years of experience of V engines to call on, for example the
famous Merlin aero engine, and the V-12 unit which powered
the Phantom III. . . . In fact the new V8 incorporated several
design features of these earlier engines.'

While crowds milled around the Silver Cloud II, Company
spokesmen stressed to official enquirers that the first V8 ran on

the test beds at Crewe five years previously, that six different types of combustion chamber were tried before the 'wedge' was finally chosen; and that in addition to bench-testing, hundreds of thousands of miles of road-testing in Europe were carried out. By the 1959 London International Motor Show, the basic price of the Silver Cloud II 4-door saloon was £4,095, or £5,802 7s. 6d. including UK purchase tax.

The original Silver Cloud (with in-line six engine) was in production from 1955 to 1958–9, the Silver Cloud II was available until 1962, when the V8 Silver Cloud III became available. Of course detail improvements were being made all the time. Last of the changes prior to the introduction of the V8 was the long-wheelbase Cloud, introduced in September 1957, in time for 1958 marketing. Conversion of the all-steel body shell was carried out by Park Ward & Co. Ltd., and although the extra length added some 1¼ cwt. to the Cloud's weight, the saloon would still (as the Conduit Street salesmen said) 'allow 100 mph to be exceeded in quiet comfort.'

When I tried my first V8 Cloud II in 1958, I timed it at 50 seconds to reach 100 mph, and the maximum was around 106. But as *The Autocar* stated in its Road Test No. 1773, 'Every year the Best Car in the World gets a little better,' and now by May, 1960, the maximum was 113·1 mph, the acceleration from standstill to 60 mph was in 11·5 secs, and the magic *ton* was reached in only 38·5 secs. I had no extensive experience of the later versions of the Cloud II, which other testers found gave a fuel consumption average of around 11·8 mpg, whereas the first V8 Cloud certainly gave 12 mpg, in itself a noticeable drop from the 16 mpg or so one could be sure of getting in the Silver Wraith days.

Even those not particularly cognisant about The Make could distinguish the Silver Cloud III from the Cloud II, since it has 'four eyes'. Or, as Conduit Street puts it: 'The Rolls-Royce Silver Cloud III has a distinctive frontal appearance which incorporates a four-headlamp system.'

But there was far more than that. The height of the radiator was slightly reduced for the Cloud III, and the bonnet top given an increased slope to improve forward vision for the driver. Wings were more highly domed, and sidelamps were moved from the top of the wing to a combined unit with the flashers, mounted on each wing nose. A power increase of about 7 per

Above The Silver Wraith is born. Clay mock-up of the front end of an experimental body for the Silver Wraith. In the production version of this body the front wings were extended into the doors. The 4,256 cc Silver Wraith with this type of body appeared in 1947

Below Testing a Silver Wraith before it goes to the customer. The routine included 14 days' testing with this Works body to check any chassis faults. Here the Acting Chief Tester is signing the three-page schedule regarding running, silence and fuel consumption

Above Facia panel of an H. J. Mulliner, Park Ward Phantom V.
Typical Rolls-Royce switchbox is in the centre of this group, with
electrical-circuit lock, and pilot indicators for generator and for low fuel
level. The four small switches above the radio are for demister, heater,
screen-washer and wiper
Below Rear view of custom-built body on the Phantom V, by Henri
Chaperon, Paris. After the limited production Phantom IV (total
production 16 cars) ended in 1956, the H. J. Mulliner, Park Ward
R.-R. Phantom V made its appearance in 1959, and the Phantom VI
in October, 1968

cent was provided from the 6,230 cc engine, the power-assisted cam-and-roller steering was modified (with extra power-assistance), and there were small but important bodywork changes including the provision of separate front seats, and a wider rear seat, with 2 in. more leg-room.

Whence came the extra power of the silver Cloud III? Among several details, the compression ratio was raised from 8·0 to 9·0:1, and larger 2-in. HD8 SU carburetters were fitted. Despite additional power-assistance for steering, it was decided to retain the factor of 4·3 turns of the wheel, lock to lock. Putting up the compression ratio seemed to do something to the fuel consumption, which during a number of tests I have made seems to average 12½ mpg, and at times to touch 16 mpg. Those with an opportunity to drive the Cloud III all-out on the track say it exceeds 117 mph. Best performance is with 100 octane fuel, which so far as overall running costs are concerned brings us back to square one, despite the improvement in fuel consumption.

In the mid-sixties, the world was a rapidly-changing place, and the question might then have been asked: 'Even if the Silver Cloud III *is* the Best Car in the World, can enough motorists afford it to make production worth while?'

The answer to this question must be in the negative if one thinks of S. B. Bailey's 'millionaires who don't even know the car uses petrol'. But let us suppose it could be shown the car is not only one of super luxury but also of extremely high performance? Might there not be very many people to whom the normal car-purchase ceiling of £2,000 or so could be raised to cover a Cloud III, assuming the car could then be kept for a decade or more? Militating against this was the classic Rolls-Royce image of a car for millionaires only. Presumably millionaires are not in much of a hurry, never have to do their motoring at Silverstone race circuit, seldom have to brake at 100 mph, or cover over 700 miles in a single day. Many drivers do make such demands, however, and it remained to be seen if this new, big, luxurious V8 was for them.

At Crewe they were becoming conscious of a number of discerning motorists who never really thought of themselves as natural Rolls-Royce owners at all. They took the car's luxury and prestige for granted, but thought its performance orthodox. The best way to show the other side of the coin would surely be to let a distinguished Grand Prix driver loose in a Cloud III. Tony Brooks accepted the challenge in 1963/4.

It was an excellent choice, for Tony Brooks had driven Frazer-Nash, Aston Martin, Connaught, BRM, Vanwall, Maserati and Ferrari. When, in 1955, he won the Syracuse Grand Prix in a Connaught, it was the first Formula 1 victory by a British car and driver for 32 years. Subsequently he won the British, Belgian, German, Italian and French Grands Prix. Thus Tony Brooks is not only one of the great Grand Prix drivers of the post-war generation, but a man with an acutely analytical approach to motoring. He accepted the challenge, laying down a number of conditions. These included the Company's agreement that he should drive the car at Goodwood, under almost racing conditions, that he should try to clock up 700 miles a day on the Continent, and take it over a gruelling section of a mountain circuit in the Alpes Maritimes; further, he should be free to make criticisms, and the Company would not delete these from any published reports. Of course they agreed.

The car tested was a perfectly standard Silver Cloud III saloon, with the 9:1 ratio 6,230-cc engine. After each section of the test, Tony Brooks tape-recorded his reactions and comments, and the following report is based on verbatim passages from these recordings.

The first test was at Goodwood, where it happened to be raining steadily. With the pools of water reflecting a heavy sky, Tony Brooks began motoring the Silver Cloud III. Soon, despite a good deal of wet-weather spray and drag, he was lapping the 2·4-mile circuit in well under two minutes, coming out of Madgwick at 78 mph, and going up to 103 before braking for St. Mary's. Rain stopped later in the day, and he then put in some fast laps, this time with four people in the car. Then he did two laps to test the braking in the severest way possible, including eight consecutive stops from about 100 mph. Altogether he completed about 20 laps.

His tape-recorded report said: 'My first impression was one of the car being extremely light to handle in relation to its size, and I was very surprised at its controllability. You could do more or less what you wanted with it, and there was no tendency to oversteer. . . . It had absolutely neutral characteristics with the tyre-pressures used. . . . I drove the car through the corners as hard as I could, and the roll for this class of car was very low indeed—and this was commented on by the track manager. We also put in some fast laps with four people up, and even with this sort of load there wasn't very much roll. I was particularly surprised at the way the car could be thrown around yet behave in such a gentlemanly way. . . .

'With four up, we stopped at from 90 to 100 mph as often as we possibly could on two successive circuits of the track. A very exacting and hard brake test, and the brakes stood up extremely well, with only a very slight tendency to fade. . . . The steering of the car was a little too low-geared for my taste, but this didn't present any real problem at Goodwood other than at the chicanes where it was necessary to cross my arms to get through in a really fast manner. The acceleration is extremely good. You can leave black marks on the road from a standing start, and with automatic transmission that is really something.'

Summing up the day's track testing, he felt the Rolls-Royce 'Came out of it with flying colours,' and 'very few standard cars, which might handle well on the roads, are quite so at home on a circuit'.

Then, with three passengers including the official photographer and observer, Tony Brooks took the Cloud III fast from Le Touquet to Cap Ferrat, 739 miles in a single day.

This is how the route-card read: 7.27 a.m., start from Le Touquet. Grey, heavy skies. Rain. Road very rough, but deserted. Cruising comfortably at speeds up to 100 mph. 8.04 a.m., Abbeville. Undulating road following the Somme valley. 8.29, Amiens. Rather more traffic. 9.27, 112 miles in two hours, following the Aisne valley. 10.10, stop for petrol at Culochy-le-Château, valley of the Marne on right. 10.27, 161 miles (49 in the hour). Roads now dry, cruising at 90–100 mph. 10.54, Sézanne. Dull road, speedo frequently at 106. 11.27, 219 miles (58 in the hour), following the Seine valley. 12.27, 278 miles (59 miles in the hour), roads now more twisting. Up to 1,922 ft over the Langres plateau. Taking bends comfortably at 90 mph. 12.47, Hairpin bends coming down to St.-Seine-l'Abbaye. 13.00, Aperitif in the garden of the Hôtellerie de Val Suzon. 'We've covered some 300 miles before lunch, putting in about 55 miles every hour. Roads have been very rough and quite twisty by French standards, but it's been a comfortable run— and effortless.' . . . 14.58, start after lunch. 15.24, petrol stop outside Dijon. 15.58, 357 miles. Following valley of the Saône.

Roads now much busier. 16.58, 418 miles (61 miles in the past hour). 17.20, Lyons. 17.58, 460 miles (42 miles in the past hour, despite very heavy traffic). Excellent road from Vienne to Valence. Speedo touches 115 mph. Strong sidewind. 18.58, 514 miles (54 miles in the hour), through quite heavy traffic. 19.10, Fuel stop at Livron. Evening sunshine. Montélimar, fair in street. Fine, dark-surfaced road. 19.58, 557 miles (43 in the hour through very heavy traffic), through Orange, vineyards of Châteauneuf-du-Pape. Now dark. Heavy lorry traffic. 20.58, 614 miles (57 in the hour). 21.58, 665 miles (51 in the hour), enter the Autoroute Estorel–Côte d'Azur. Deserted. Speedo reaches 120 mph on downhill section. Stop from 90 mph to avoid tanker pulling into our lane. 22.58, 726 miles (61 miles in the hour), Cagnes, stop for petrol. 23.15, Nice, Promenade des Anglais. 23.27, Grand Hôtel du Cap Ferrat. End of journey. 739 miles.

Tony Brooks commented: 'We've covered roughly 740 miles, and I can honestly say that I'm good for many more miles of motoring yet. I've never arrived at the end of a similar journey less tired . . . and we haven't had an easy run. We had rough and then fairly twisty roads early in the journey; heavy traffic for about four hours after lunch, and finally about three hours of night driving. We are still all pretty fresh. It has been effortless high-speed travel, and this aspect of the car impresses me enormously. . . . The steering is very impressive. . . . Many power steering systems are effortless, but you lose all sense of contact with the road, which of course can be very dangerous in slippery conditions. This can't happen with a Rolls-Royce. . . . The car really digs in on corners. In fact, with the tyre pressures I used you can corner remarkably fast on any kind of corner: I have not sampled better road-holding in a luxury saloon. . . . I particularly liked the over-ride control of the automatic gearbox because I could, for example, put it in third and hold it there as long as I wanted. This made overtaking so much quicker. . . . On the autoroute at night the car was impressive at very high speeds. The autoroute is far from straight, and full of very fast curves, many of which we took at over 100 mph. . . . One simply set the car up in a corner and left it to do the rest. . . . You felt you were floating along as if on a magic carpet. A little tyre noise and wind were all that could be heard. We covered a lot of ground very quickly. . . .'

In the Alpes Maritimes, fast mountain motoring is an excellent test of the braking, steering, balance and acceleration of any car, so Tony Brooks took the Cloud III over the kind of circuit that has been used as an elimination run in the Monte Carlo rally. They left Monte Carlo and drove over the circuit La Turbie–Laghet–la Trinité–Drap–l'Escarène–col de Braus–Sospel–Castillion–Menton, and back to Monte Carlo. In particular they made a fast ascent of the col de Braus, stopped at the top for photography, then made an all-out descent to Sospel on a comparatively clear road. This descent includes some 30 consecutive corners and *lacets* (tight hairpins) separated by short stretches of straight. In many of these straights, Tony Brooks took the car up to around 70 mph, braked, flung the car round, accelerating hard out of the bends. The 2-ton Cloud III rushed down the 3,287-ft col almost continuously on left or right-hand lock, taking a corner very fast every few seconds . . . 'At the bottom we pulled in to a garage for petrol. Smoke was pouring from the brake drums, and the garage lad reached for a bucket of water. No need. In fact, the brakes had never grabbed nor shown any appreciable sign of fade. We motored on over the rest of the course. . . .'

At the end of this test Tony Brooks reported: 'Despite these tight hairpins, it was quite easy to get the car round even if you approached them very fast and got a little bit of understeer. On many cars of this size one would have found it very difficult. There was always ample lock to spare, and this gave the car manoeuvrability. The overriding manual control of the gearbox was extremely useful under these conditions. I could play between third and second all the way up the Cols. I could keep it in third and change down to second for really tight hairpins.'

His final verdict, after living with the Silver Cloud III for two weeks and driving it far and fast for 2,700 miles, was summed up in these words: 'The pleasure that I found in driving the Silver Cloud came from a balance of qualities that is unique in my experience. . . . The surprising thing to me is how well adapted the car is to modern traffic conditions. Indeed, it tends to solve many contemporary motoring problems. Motoring of this kind cannot be anything but expensive, but I would say that in terms of sheer motoring pleasure, safety and durability, the Rolls-Royce is excellent value for £5,500. As a big, luxurious car that can nevertheless be driven in a highly sporting manner, there is nothing quite like it.'

There is a postscript. This Cloud III, after the necessarily severe handling it received in the test, had a routine service which included renewing the tyres and relining brakes. A few days later it was driven to Munich to take part in the British Week, in which it was used for VIP transport. Afterwards it underwent full road tests by the French *l'Auto-Journal* and by a series of British newspapers.

After the Continent testing, Tony Brooks had a lengthy interview with Mr. Grylls, and when the tape of this discussion was transcribed it ran to some 14,000 words, or about a quarter of the total length of this book. The interview was completely frank, and in the course of it some criticisms of design features were made, to which the Chief Engineer was able to explain the Rolls-Royce policy. The ordinary owner of a Silver Cloud III would never need to drive his car in the deliberately brutal method which an official tester must adopt.

The following extracts of the interview are my own edited sections containing perhaps rather more of the criticism than the car's outstanding performance in Tony Brooks' hands might seem to warrant. But a good many people automatically genuflect every time Rolls and Royce are mentioned, and this tends to obliterate the fact that if the car is The Best Car in the World, it is on that pinnacle only because of a continuing policy of engineering development—a policy which must be sparked off with scientific, factual criticism.

The dialogue went as follows. Tony Brooks opened by saying: 'I should really preface all these comments with the point that I have driven this car not as an average Rolls-Royce owner would, but in a decidedly sporting manner. From this point of view I found the change down to second on our particular car not very smooth. If I was behind traffic, and pottering along at about 20 mph in top, then all of a sudden the road would become clear. I would press the accelerator to the floor and the car would lurch forward.'

'This is the biggest unsolved problem in our particular form of automatic transmission,' explained Mr. Grylls. (*Remember, this interview took place while the present Silver Shadow was under development.*) 'We have retained a stepped transmission having the least possible slip because we think this is the most suited to motoring in Europe. Of course, any transmission needs a little time to bed down: the car you tested, I think, was a new one.'

'Yes, it had done 500 miles when I took it over. It's certainly true that a Bentley I drove the other day was smoother on that particular gear change. And of course the situation can be avoided by moving the lever into third position; then you're ready with the power available immediately the road is clear—and this works very well. But there's another criticism here. Between second and third from the point of view of ultimate performance, there's too big a gap—particularly if you happen to hit the change up on a hill. The fall-off in acceleration is very noticeable as you get into third.'

'Only "very noticeable," I would say, if you are particularly brutal with the throttle,' commented Mr. Grylls.

'It was deliberate, of course. But is there no possible way of closing down the second to third gap?'

'There is no *reasonable* way of closing down the gap. You see, you have these four ratios in a total of three epicyclic trains, and the fluid flywheel actually moves up and down the box. Although geographically it's in the front, it's in the middle of the box in some of these ratios.'

'But surely a torque-converter overcomes this, doesn't it?'

'It does in that with three ratios you get almost as good a coverage. But you can't drive at full throttle in top gear at low speeds as you can with our type of transmission. We can get down to 900 rev/min in top gear before changing down, but we can manually select third gear for acceleration or braking when desired. A torque-converter necessarily burns more fuel.' (*As we shall see in Chapter Nine, a number of transmission changes have been made for the Silver Shadow, for home and export markets.*)

Continued Tony Brooks: 'It does seem a pity that the design of the new engine has produced rather a noisy tick-over. Couldn't this be reduced—even though it is quickly lost on moving off from rest?'

'This is inherently more difficult with an aluminium engine, and so far we have not found a satisfactory answer.' (*Again, there has been continuing development for the power-unit of the Silver Shadow.*)

'The next point I've got down here is the steering, which I thought was really first-class. But from my own point of view, from the sporting side, I thought it was unnecessarily low-geared.'

'We think this is the best compromise. You *can* drive in a

sporting way with this ratio, as you've discovered. And at the same time less continuous attention is needed under normal circumstances. We describe this as having a "low sneeze-factor." '

(*The power-assisted steering of the Silver Shadow includes Saginaw recirculatory-ball-type operation, with an integral hydraulic damper. Hydraulic pressure for steering assistance comes from a Hobourn-Eaton pump belt-driven from the crankshaft. A torsion-bar-operated valve controls the pressure.*)

'There's one thing I'm pretty sure you will disagree with me about, and that is the question of tyre pressures. I found the differential of your standard pressures too great for fast road work. I preferred 25 front, 28 rear for normal touring.'

'I only disagree with you because there's all the difference between going for an ordinary run to London, and driving as you've been driving. And I should add that the tyres we manage to achieve now are safe at recommended pressures even if driven all-out continuously.'

'Let's turn to the hard and soft ride control. All it's doing is to give you a stiffer movement at the rear of the car if you've got a heavy load. But it seemed to me from the cornering point of view it was upsetting the balance of the car. Couldn't one have this switch operating on all four shock-absorbers so that one has an honest-to-goodness hard ride, as opposed to a compromise?'

'It is a compromise only if you judge it from a severely sporting point of view. With the present system you have the kind of ride that most people expect from a Rolls-Royce and, as you'll agree, you *can* drive the car in a very enterprising way if you want to.' (*There is no switch-controlled variation of 'Ride' in the Silver Shadow, but an automatic hydraulic height-control system is provided, ensuring optimum ride and handling characteristics under all normal weight and road conditions.*)

'I found the brakes of the car wonderful,' continued Tony Brooks. 'But they do bring up the obvious question of discs, and their even greater resistance to fade. Hasn't it been possible yet to overcome their incidental drawbacks?'

'As you know,' replied Mr. Grylls, 'discs do have advantages over conventional drum brakes. They have better heat-dissipating qualities and so show less fade under continual high-speed use. But our drum brakes are far from conventional. The Rolls-Royce arrangement of trailing shoes at the front and equal-wearing shoes at the rear is less temperature-sensitive than disc brakes. When you combine this with heavy ribbing of the brake drums, and a very large brake lining area and specially-developed linings, brake fade has ceased to be a problem. Our tests in fact have shown that we can stop once a minute from 70 mph until the linings are worn out. And of course pedal pressure is no problem in a Rolls-Royce because we give you servo assistance that makes you seven times the man you are!'

'Yes, but what are the disadvantages of discs?'

'Disc braking systems are usually heavier. They are inclined to be noisy in operation at certain speeds, and their performance often varies in different climatic conditions. And their rate of wear is at least twice. In other words, you would have to reline them twice as often as our brakes. And the discs which wear comparatively well tend to squeak. All of which we'll overcome one day. But we won't fit discs until they are as silent and smooth and progressive as the brakes we have now.' (*Mr. Grylls was as good as his word. Even while this interview was being recorded, Crewe was developing the disc braking system of Rolls-Royce Girling, adopted in 1965 for the Silver Shadow.*)

'Right,' persisted Tony Brooks. 'Then let's turn to suspension. I found it very good. But there was a slight tendency for the car to wander at speed, particularly noticeable on the rough French roads, in spite of our 5 lb pressure differential between front and rear tyres when cold. Was this perhaps partly due to the large suspension movements?'

'Self-centring which is essential in a motor-car is incompatible with complete freedom from wander. Incidentally the tyre pressure differential when hot is about 8 lb.'

'Surely independent rear suspension would further improve the ride and road-holding?'

'Well, it's simply not true that i.r.s. is the answer to every ride problem. Take the swing-axle type which is the commonest of all. It can lead to some very tricky handling characteristics. . . . Of course there are other forms, but they all pose problems, of wear and noise, which just aren't acceptable when you're designing to Rolls-Royce standards. . . . Our cars are heavy, they're capable of travelling at very high speeds, and they have to be very comfortable. Consequently the suspension has to be fairly soft and you have to cater for considerable vertical movements. No present independent rear system could handle all this as well as our system does.' (*Again, research and development were taking place at the time. Crewe finally developed an independent rear suspension system for the Silver Shadow with coil-sprung single fabricated trailing arms, plus telescopic dampers, the arms being angled to give slight negative camber of the tyre tread during fast cornering.)*

In other parts of the taped interview which so far have remained confidential in Crewe's files Tony Brooks had a number of other minor points to make, some of which he agreed were matters of personal preference, and many of which have been dealt with in the design of the Silver Shadow. He felt that amendments to the layout of the dash, and the inclusion of additional protective padding could be made. He found one aspect of rearward visibility slightly difficult when driving on the right-hand side of the road. He also remarked on the travel of the handbrake lever, the performance of the screenwipers at very high road speeds, and the noise made by the air scoop in the scuttle, and of the ventilation fans. He said he would have preferred louder horns on a test of this nature.

As the qualities of Rolls-Royce are to be seen not only in the performance of a new car, but in the way that performance is maintained over the years, Tony Brooks was invited to give a tough test to a six-year old car while the experience of the S.3 was still vividly in mind. So he selected a Bentley S.1 (equivalent of the Silver Cloud) from a London showroom. This car was first registered in 1957, had 40,000 miles to its credit, and was priced at £2,650. Among his detailed comments were: 'It's very difficult to detect any real deterioration in performance . . . Of course you're saving yourself something like £3,000 compared with a new car. . . . The brakes are good, rather heavier than on the S.3, but I'm sure well up to S.1 standard. . . . I think the wheels are a shade out of balance' (*new tyres had been fitted*) 'because we had a little vibration on the steering, but that's all. . . .'

With the whole series of Clouds, the question does arise as to how the various models may be dated. From the used-car point of view it is important to know when specification changes were made in the Clouds. Naturally the only certain method of finding the age of a Rolls-Royce is by checking the guarantee date; in some instances customers may have some of the noteworthy 'dating' features fitted to their cars after delivery. Nevertheless, here is a list of salient specification changes.

SILVER CLOUD

April, 1955. Introduction with larger engine, 4,887 cc. New cylinder head and porting. New body, chassis, smaller diameter wheels, 15-in. Automatic transmission standardised.

April, 1956. Introduction of twin master cylinders. Two brake fluid reservoirs under bonnet.

July, 1956. Splayed frame. Front extensions to chassis frame splayed outwards, whereas previous frames had parallel extensions.

December, 1956. Minor wiring change, so brake lights cut out when the flasher is working—on the same side as that particular flasher.

February, 1957. Provision of summer/winter heater water taps under bonnet.

September, 1957. Engine compression ratio raised to 8·0:1. Carburetter choke size changed from $1\frac{3}{4}$ in. to 2-in.

April, 1958. Twin jet centrally mounted windscreen washer.

May, 1958. Substitution of hollow type front-suspension yokes by solid type. These latter can be recognised by external oil pipes on the yokes.

April, 1959. Pressure cap fitted to top of radiator header tank on refrigerated cars. Blanking plate fitted in lieu of pressure cap on non-refrigerated cars.

SILVER CLOUD II

September, 1959. Introduction. V8 engine, revised heating system incorporating capping-rail outlet ducts, and a re-circulatory system. Power-assisted steering standard.

October, 1960. Spare-wheel cover plate, fresh-air duct under left-hand wing entering car below dash. Capping rail air ducts fitted with chrome-plated handles. Cigar lighter illuminates when instruments are on, and lighter is withdrawn. Extension speaker on rear parcel shelf, with balance control, fitted as standard.

October, 1961. Combined headlamp flasher and indicator switch, switch for rear window demister and handbrake warning light fitted on facia panel. Blue illumination for instruments. Sliding doors to front door pockets. Central heater duct to the rear. Provision for ram air demist.

March, 1962. Interior of boot painted black in all models.

May, 1962. Larger rear-lamp assembly.

August, 1962, Sealed-beam headlamps. No RR monogram inside lamps.

SILVER CLOUD III

October, 1962. Introduction. Lowered bonnet line, restyled front wings, with four headlamps. Engine now 9:1 compression ratio. Carburetter choke 2-in. dia. Distributor incorporating vacuum advance/retard mechanism. Improved power-assisted steering. Individual front seats as standard. RR monogram on boot.

April, 1963. Change from chrome-plated to stainless steel wheel discs.

May, 1963. Wiper-blade stops fitted below windscreen.

August, 1963. Small pulley attached to chassis frame, below the starter motor, to improve efficiency of handbrake.

November, 1963. More effective demister. Width of demister panel itself reduced from 2 ft 10 in. to 2 ft 6 in.

January, 1964. Heat-shield fitted on right-hand exhaust manifold. Wider rear seat fitted to standard-wheelbase saloons only.

March, 1964. Restyled headlamp surround incorporating RR monogram.

May, 1964. Wide rims to rear wheels on standard and long-wheelbase cars for the UK and European markets only.

June, 1964. Additional fresh-air control knob, repositioned adjacent to the steering column.

September, 1964. Nemag speedometer. Zero mph marked on dial commences at approximately 7 o'clock position, as distinct from the 1.0 o'clock zero position on the previous type of speedometer.

And then, in October, 1965, came the introduction of the Silver Shadow and Bentley T series.

Eight

THE PHANTOMS

M UCH myth and legend has grown up around the Phantom
IV. Every Rolls-Royce enthusiast knows it as the 'Royal'
series of straight-eights which succeeded the V12 Phantom III,
and it may be recalled that the Phantom IV was in extremely
limited production from 1950 to 1956, that versions produced from
1952 had automatic transmission (some earlier cars were modified), and that the total production was not much more than a
baker's dozen.

'Wars usually make one change one's policy,' said Mr. Grylls
to the Institution of Mechanical Engineers, 'and in a direction
to counter monetary inflation. A possible successor to the Phantom III car, using the straight-eight, was never made in large
numbers,[1] but was limited to 12 for royal persons and rulers
of states. . . .'

This figure 12 is indefinite. It may have been 18. A number
of Phantom III's were converted to straight-eights, using modified B-range engines (this conversion is not one necessarily
approved by the Company), but these are not true Phantom IV's.

As I have related in *The Book of the Phantoms:* 'Chassis modifications were made to Royal order, and the cars supplied to
members of the British Royal Family went out with a pair of
special-edition Instruction Books—one in grey leather, with
red-and-gold lettering, on the front seat, and a de-luxe edition
bound in white leather on the rear seat! These books, today
among the most prized of collectors' car literature, show such
details as individual Royal lamps and coachwork wiring.'

HM the Queen took delivery of her Phantom IV when she was
Princess Elizabeth. A seven-passenger limousine was ordered

---

[1] The power unit was that mentioned by Mr. Grylls in his 'History of a Dimension': 'In addition to this new (B-range) six cylinder engine it had been
decided to make a four-cylinder and a straight-eight. . . . The war prevented
any immediate sale of these engines, but an immense mileage was piled up in
vehicles run as staff cars or converted to lorries.'

by HRH the Duchess of Kent, and HRH the Duke of Gloucester favoured a streamlined Hooper carriage of distinctly sporting lines. HH the Aga Khan was an early Phantom IV enthusiast, with a rather heavy Hooper sedanca-de-ville, King Faisal chose a Hooper limousine not unlike that of the Duke of Gloucester, and the Maharaja of Mysore commissioned James Young to build a sporting, whitewall-tyred drophead coupe. Most of the cars on the Phantom IV chassis gave the appearance of considerable length, but HM the Shah of Iran ordered from H. J. Mulliner a compact and quite sporting drophead coupe.

The Duke of Edinburgh, though not primarily a Rolls-Royce man, is mentioned by Helen Cathcart in *HRH Prince Philip, Sportsman* (Stanley Paul): ' . . . he elected to drive for a time in an exclusive and unashamedly opulent royal Rolls. No Rolls-Royce quite like it, indeed, had ever been seen before. The prototype had been under test for five years, becoming familiarly known as the Scalded Cat for its speed and quick get-away, and Prince Philip specially visited the Works to see his model under construction.

'The car was classed as a Phantom IV 5·7 litre straight-eight, the first eight-cylinder-in-line Rolls-Royce had ever built, readily capable of 130 mph in top, and equally astonishing at that time in performance in other respects. Outwardly it was a limousine of supreme elegance, of razor-edge lines, finished—with more than twenty coats of paint—in what has since come to be known as Edinburgh green. . . .' The car mentioned was later repainted maroon, and used as one of the State Rolls-Royces. The number-plate was then removed (it had been registered as LGO 10), since no official cars of the Monarch carry Excise licences nor Road Fund registration. The Phantom IV was the chief State car of the Queen until 1960.

Although Phantom IV's in their day were sold as Mr. Grylls said 'to royal persons and rulers of states', there was at one period a policy proposed at Crewe that the straight-eight should come on to the market in the normal way. One can only assume that the success of the Silver Wraith and the development of the V8 engine made the progress of a straight-eight policy commercially impossible to complete.

What, then, *is* the Phantom IV? Fundamentally it is a 145-in. wheelbase car, the overall length of which is not quoted since all the coachwork was to special order. Front track is 58½ in., rear track is 63-in. General chassis construction of course is similar to that of the Silver Wraith. Front suspension is of course independent, with open helical springs and hydraulic shock dampers. There are two upper and two lower radius arms of different lengths set at a leading angle, between which a vertical yoke is carried, and on this the stub-axles are pivoted. Ball joints and steering pivot bearings are lubricated from the central chassis system. To reduce any tendency to roll, a steel torsion-rod stabiliser is provided at the front-end, this being carried in rubber bearings and coupled to the wheel mountings with rubber pads. Rear suspension is by semi-elliptics in combination with controllable shock-dampers. These are of the classic Rolls-Royce pre-War type, operated by a knob above the steering wheel over a sector from 'Normal' to 'Hard.'

The rear shock dampers themselves consist of a piston-operated assembly working in a cylinder which is maintained full of oil, the latter being displaced from one end of the cylinder to the other (by rear-axle movement) past spring-loaded valves. The loading of these valves, and hence the degree of damping, is controllable through the ride-control lever by a small pump carried in a casing bolted to the gearbox, which maintains a pressure of oil in a system of piping. This pressure is variable, and is controlled through a relief valve operated by the 'Normal/Hard' lever. The pump is charged with oil from the gearbox, but no oil from this source is actually pumped into the dampers. It is simply use of gearbox oil to regulate on the loading the shock-damper valves.

The Phantom IV's rear axle is of the semi-floating type, with hypoid gears, and the whole braking system is similar to that of the Silver Wraith, having hydraulic operation on front drums, mechanical operation on the rear, assisted by the mechanically-driven friction motor. Steering is Marles cam-and-roller type, and the detachable steel disc wheels are shod with 8·00 by 17 Dunlop Fort 'C' tyres.

Of course as one looks today at the Phantom IV as a collector's piece, interest centres chiefly on the straight-eight power unit. This is a monobloc casting with detachable head, overhead inlet, side exhaust valves, of $3\frac{1}{2}$ in. bore, $4\frac{1}{2}$ in. stroke, giving a capacity of 5,675 cc. There is pressure-feed to all crankshaft and connecting-rod bearings, from a $2\frac{1}{4}$-gallon sump, and the usual Rolls-Royce type of relief valve providing positive low-pressure supply to the valve rocker shaft, from which the inlet valves, push-rods and tappets are lubricated. A single duplex Stromberg downdraught carburetter is used, with a manifold system based on that of the B-80 engine.

The rear axle ratio is 4·25:1, and the first series of Phantom IV's with a manual box gave ratios of 12·74:1 (top), 8·52, 5·71 and 4·25:1 respectively.

Unlike the Phantom III, which had manual overriding control of ignition advance on the steering column (making a total of three knobs on the column), the Phantom IV relied on the automatic advance-retard mechanism in the distributor body, so there are only two controls above the steering wheel, the ride control and throttle respectively. Firing order of the straight-eight is 1, 6, 2, 5, 8, 3, 7, 4, No. 1 being the front. The handsome radiator block has the old-style thermostatically-operated radiator shutters. The car was delivered with an anti-freeze coolant mixture intended for all-year-round use, and shutters open and close to maintain a running temperature in the 75–85-deg.C range.

As rare-book collectors nowadays find extremely high prices are reached in the saleroom for Phantom IV handbooks, it should be noted there are several editions, even for the manual-gearbox version of the 'Royal' car. Naturally because of its scarcity every Phantom IV handbook has considerable value. Most of the few in circulation are No. XV. Of even greater rarity, however, is No. XIV. Pages from this were reproduced in *The Book of the Phantoms*. Mechanical details are identical, but the colour-coded electrical wiring charts of the truly royal book show the additional coachbuilders' wiring for the roof motor, Piper blind unit, and for special flood-lights. There is an intriguing difference, too, between Fig. 53 in the 'royal' book and the nearly similar photograph in the ordinary Phantom IV series XV book. In the earlier book the top of the windscreen carries the special mauve indicator lamp used by the Royal Family.

In 1959, with the advent of the 6¼-litre V8 engine, there came the Phantom V and, almost inevitably, a new series of Phantoms for Royalty.

All that we have seen in the preceding chapters regarding the development of the Cloud-type chassis and the V8 engine came to a particular fulfilment in September, 1959, with the Phantom V, the largest Rolls-Royce ever built. Compared with the Silver

Above Royal Rolls-Royces are depicted on this page. The Phantom V
supplied to HM the Queen soon after the introduction of this series
(she had previously owned a Phantom IV) was equipped by Park Ward
with special coachwork including full air-conditioning, relay-operated
coachwork features such as sliding roof panel, and fluorescent-strip
interior lighting for State occasions

Below A Phantom V supplied to HM Queen Elizabeth the Queen
Mother has this unique landaulette coachwork by H. J. Mulliner, Park
Ward. There are the usual air-conditioning ducts, communication
system, and remote electric control of division and windows

Two views of the V-8 engine and automatic transmission unit of the Phantom V, first introduced in 1959, although the aluminium V-8 engine was in development back in 1947. Subsequent changes included a new head design with improved breathing, and spark plugs brought up above the exhaust manifold. There is now finger-tip electric control of the automatic shift mechanism

Cloud, the wheelbase is 144 in. (one inch shorter than the Phantom IV), but the general construction is such that it is possible for coach builders to achieve a limousine body with an unusually spacious rear compartment, making it suitable for use by companies and corporations. The front track is just over 2·8 in. wider, and 4 in. wider at the rear; and although the front suspension used a number of S.2 components, the forged, swept-back front wishbones are 1-in. longer; there are differences, also, in the rear suspension. For example, no Z-bar was used on the first-series Phantom V's, as on the S.2. Autostatic Girling type brakes are used, the shoe remaining in contact with the drums, and for the P-V the Rolls-Royce brake philosophy of 'front-two-trailing, rear trailing-and-leading' was maintained.

The first two Phantom V's introduced at the 1959 International Motor Show were a Park Ward enclosed limousine in black, with tan hide at the front and the rear compartment in fawn cloth, and a James Young touring limousine in velvet green, with beige hide at the front and beige cloth for the rear. The overall length of the P-V chassis being 19 ft 10 in. (6·045 m), the James Young designers were able to evolve a styling giving maximum comfort no matter whether the car is owner- or chauffeur-driven. Construction is of steel and light alloy to give exceptional strength and lightness. All the interior panelling is of aluminium. The front screen, electrically-controlled division and the rear window are of Triplex glass, curved to give full vision. All four glasses are power-operated, and the screen and rear window are fitted with electric demisters. Total UK price of the Park Ward enclosed limousine in 1959 was £8,904 17s. 6d., and £9,110 5s. 10d. for the James Young.

As the largest and best of the Rolls-Royce range, it came in for much praise and a few criticisms when it was first seen. In the *Sunday Express*, for example, Robert Glenton praised the Phantom V for its general excellence, and in his 'Glenton's Score Card' commented: 'There is nothing to do but sprinkle *Ten out of Ten* with every glittering adjective that comes to mind.' However, in his review he did rightly point out that: 'The most incredible things about this car are two arrogances, so incon-spicuous that they are hidden under the bonnet. Imagine delving into the huge boot, dragging out the jack, raising a front wheel, taking it off, unscrewing eleven nuts, removing a panel . . . and all for why? *Just to change a plug.* This car has a

V8 engine, so if the faulty plug is not on that side you have to go round the car and start all over again. . . . And that's not all. To put in more oil one has to remove the whole foundation of the air-conditioning. Rolls-Royce are apt to look at you blandly and say: '*But why should you want to change a plug? And surely you don't change the oil YOURSELF?*'

Of course this was only intended as a light-hearted comment, and, as we have seen, a number of modifications were made during the years. Among other things, the plug positions were altered. Unfortunately due to international conditions the cost was rising all the time. Following the introduction of the Phantom V in 1959, a new Park Ward seven-passenger limousine was supplied to HM the Queen in the spring of 1960. This caused world comment, due to the excellence of the car and its coachwork, and by 1965 Rolls-Royce included in their list 'a Phantom V specially designed for Ceremonial Occasions.' The list price of the standard H. J. Mulliner, Park Ward seven-passenger limousine was now £9,571, including UK purchase-tax, the basic price being £7,875. And although not priced, the 'Phantom V State limousine' was generally believed to be considerably more expensive, since the coachwork features, all optional, were designed regardless of cost or complexity.

Details of this (marketed) limousine 'for Ceremonial occasions' are not identical with those of the car supplied in 1960 to the Royal Mews. A special feature of the 1965 car is the hydraulically-operated folding roof to the rear compartment, giving the maximum possible visibility. The rear seat can be raised electrically by 3½-in., and there is fluorescent strip lighting in the rear compartment. The chassis specification is similar to that of the Phantom V limousine, but the State landaulette is fitted with *two* refrigeration units, one for the chauffeur's compartment, the other for the rear passengers.

The Royal Phantom V by Park Ward has the rear part of the roof panelled in one large Perspex moulding. The front section of the roof to the rear compartment is of glass. There are electrically-operated sliding panels covering the glass and Perspex sections when privacy is required, and the back section of the dome is covered with an aluminium structure lined with plastic and with West of England cloth to match the rest of the rear interior lining. This dome takes about one minute to close for privacy. Wool mohair rugs, walnut curl veneer cross-banded with French walnut; and the chauffeur's compartment trimmed in dark blue cloth.

This Royal car looks rather larger than it is. Overall length is a fraction under 19 ft. 9 in., and the height to the top of the Perspex dome is 6 ft 1 in. The whole lower section of the body panelling is, in fact, an entirely standard Park Ward structure. There appears to be a very commodious luggage compartment, but in fact most of this space is taken up with the panels used to cover the glass and transparent plastic when the Queen is travelling privately.

Two rather personal questions are frequently asked regarding the use of this Royal Phantom V. *'If the car won't take luggage, then where is it stacked?'* and *'When this great car goes on tour, where do they garage it?'*

The answer to the first query is that when travelling between Royal residences, the Phantom V may be seen accompanied by a small station-waggon packed full of luggage. And the answer to the second query is known to a number of police officials who, when a Royal visit with an overnight stay is planned, arrange to garage the State Phantom V in police premises.

In October 1968, when the Phantom V had been in series production for nine years (including the Phantom V Mark II), the Phantom VI was introduced. By now the price-tag was £10,050 for the seven-passenger H. J. Mulliner Park Ward enclosed limousine. In the UK there was the additional purchase tax burden of £2,793. As we shall see in the next chapter, the Silver Cloud-series engine underwent continuing development. A new cylinder-head giving better flow was introduced for the aluminium V8 power unit. This was used for the Silver Shadow and, from 1968, for the Phantom VI. A special coachwork innovation for the 'VI' is the use of two entirely separate air-conditioning units, the rear-compartment being served by its own additional unit in the luggage boot.

Nine

SYBARITIC SHADOWS

FLEET STREET's world of newspapers was slightly knocked off balance in September, 1965, when Crewe announced the introduction of the revolutionary Rolls-Royce Silver Shadow and the Bentley T series.

It is no secret that Fleet Street looks at any new car through a curious perspective often distorted by the number of pages of supporting advertising it hopes to get in the next appropriation from the car manufacturer. But with Rolls-Royce, it's different. Anything so sensational as the Silver Shadow is headline news.

The Times (British Motoring Survey) ran a detailed interview with Shadwell Harry Grylls, the Chief Engineer and chief architect of the Silver Shadow's design team. ('These new cars come at the end of $10\frac{1}{2}$ years in which the Rolls-Royce Silver Clouds and the Bentley S series achieved a high reputation all over the world,' *The Times* said. 'The new cars represent a radical advance . . .')

Mr. Grylls disclosed some of his own problems. 'A stylist does not design cars *in vacuo*,' he asserted. 'Every model of a future car provides for a particular size of passenger compartment and allows for those inevitable pieces of machinery that move the compartment about. . . . The Englishman's requirements are precise—a smaller car with a better performance, with more room in it, with a larger boot, with no sacrifice for these ends. The American's requirements are less easy to describe. Overall external size is of no importance. A soft ride is essential; the steering must be finger-light and the car extremely stable. The mainland of Europe wants first-class road-holding, good cornering and indestructible brakes. The problem is to combine all this in one car. It can be done . . .'

The *Sunday Times* (Maxwell Boyd) commented: 'Production of the Silver Shadow was slow getting into gear, partly because of the problems of teaching old hands new and complex techniques on the line. Assembly has now reached over 20 cars a week. There is an 18-month waiting-list at home, and half that overseas, indicating a fairly healthy world demand. Rolls-Royce themselves were particularly sensitive over the Shadow because of the threat of Germany's Mercedes 600. But they can be reassured. There is room for *two* best cars in the world—and the Silver Shadow is undoubtedly one of them. It is also the only one with the Rolls-Royce radiator.'

Commented Elizabeth Benson under the same banner: 'It is big but not *too* big for those who want the supreme status symbol while not desiring to look like refugees from the *corps diplomatique* or property developers. It *is* rather more modern—both in front-end appearance and in its ego-buttering innards—yet it still has Roycean dignity. It can, dare one say it, be regarded as a family car, because it is not *too* ostentatious. It is nice to know that if you own the necessary bullion you need not have the trad polished-wood interior of the car I tested. Any interior finish can be yours.'

Unhappily a finish of a different sort awaited *The Observer*'s Gordon Wilkins, formerly Technical Editor of *Autocar*, motoring correspondent of *The Observer* for ten years when the Silver Shadow came out, one of the most experienced journalists in the car-testing game. He gave the Shadow a gruelling test on the Continent, and at the end of a 350-mile run to Milan, cruising at 90–100 mph, found that one of the hydraulic fluid reservoirs down to the minimum mark, and the other falling. One of the front levelling jacks had sprung a leak.

'The Milan agents instantly produced all the parts required,' said Gordon Wilkins, 'fitting a new levelling jack, new seals to both hydraulic pumps, cured the engine oil leak, and fitted a new electric motor to the driver's door window, which had stuck open. . . . This may sound quite a catalogue of trouble, even on a car which had done 18,000 miles of hard and often brutal test driving, but another thousand miles of hard driving was covered without further trouble. . . . To meet the exacting demands of wealthy connoisseurs the top cars are becoming extremely complex and it may be that in future they will be like private aeroplanes which, as a matter of course, need highly skilled, regular and expensive maintenance. . . .'

Of course it is not suggested that under routine driving the Silver Shadow needs regular and expensive maintenance. But the car *is* complex. As *Autocar* put it; The Shadow: 'conceals

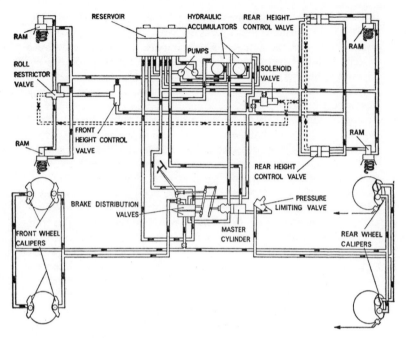

Schematic layout of the Silver Shadow hydraulic system,
showing braking and height-control circuits

beneath an almost austerely orthodox new body a wealth of
mechanical innovation. In fact, it possesses more individuality
and advanced engineering than this company has ever displayed
before in a new model.'

As originally introduced, the Silver Shadow features a monocoque (chassis-less) steel body shell with separate front and rear
sub-frames and suspension assemblies, all-independent suspension
with automatic hydraulic height control, four-wheel disc brakes
operated by dual high-pressure hydraulic systems, a modified
all-aluminium V8 engine, with electric operation of the overriding controls for the automatic transmission system.

The Company's own description of the Shadow and the
Bentley T explained that these new models 'Are the result of
more than ten years of continuous development by Rolls-Royce
engineers paying meticulous attention to detail which is part of

the Company's tradition. . . . The specification, which is as advanced and comprehensive as available, includes a triplicated power braking system . . .'

Within the private confines of some departments at Crewe they were less reverential about the new series which for reasons which are neither here nor there, resulted in it being known as the T version of the Bentley. They dubbed both Rolls and Bentley 'Henry's Model T,' disregarding the fact that the 'H' in S. H. Grylls' name stands for Harry.

Before considering the final Silver Shadow specification, one must go the source, to Mr. Grylls himself, to see how the Company's design policy operated during these vital years of development. Why had they now turned to disc brakes, to independent suspension, to a complexity of electric and hydraulic regulators? The following brief edited extracts of *The Times* interview tell why.

'Independent rear suspension (i.r.s.) is gaining ground in Europe, but is not yet used by Detroit. A softer rear suspension was essential (in engineers' language at least 12 in. static deflection) . . . A decision was made to go all the way and incorporate i.r.s. The rear wheels could now be properly located and given any desired motion in their rise and fall. Indirect advantages ensued because the rear axle centre case and the propeller shaft no longer moved up and down. Of all the possible i.r.s. linkages, the trailing arm seemed to take up the least valuable space and could most easily be given anti-dive properties when braking.

'Difficulties were expected with road noise, axle noise and transmission jerks. The trailing arms are pivoted on rubber bushes attached to a local sub-frame. Both this sub-frame and the rear-axle case had to be insulated from the steel body shell. After some trials of rubber mounts, all-metal ones were chosen because they could provide more damping than any known rubber or such-like material. . . . A consequence of i.r.s. is that short axle shafts replace, for accommodation of vertical movement, the normal much longer propeller shaft. In order that the Hooke's joints may normally run at an average angle of zero, suspension levelling is required.

'The styling department were overjoyed. Soft springs no longer made a car look silly when laden or not laden—ordinarily both cannot look right. Front-suspension levelling similarly removed the only disadvantage of soft springs. The headlamps would now always aim correctly. Levelling needs a source of high-pressure oil, which was in any case available because of a new braking system. . . . Height sensors (or "pussies' whiskers") measure the position of the suspension and call on the oil pressure supply to move the top-end of the spring, the floor being the same distance from the ground, whatever the load may be . . .

'The front suspension is new, containing anti-dive geometry, and is pivoted by rubber bushes on a sub-frame flexibly attached again by resilient metal mounts, to the body. . . . A re-circulating ball-and-nut integral ram power steering is mounted on the sub-frame and steers through a linkage of almost perfect geometry.

'A factor for consideration was whether the time had come to alter the servo-assisted brake system, which had been a feature of Rolls-Royce cars since 1925. It was becoming increasingly difficult to put the friction servo between the floor and the ground; even in its latest form there was a slight lag in operation of a few inches, and rods essentially operated the rear brakes, the linkage being almost unprotectable from the salt, now a feature of motorways. . . . The nicest arrangement seemed a duplicated full servo system distributed so that a failure of either system leaves the car with both front and rear braking. The energy for the servo comes from two separate engine-driven pumps supplying separate accumulators, receiving their instruction from separate valves moved by the brake pedal. After standing for a long time, both accumulators could be empty. A third direct hydraulic system was therefore included, operating half the rear brakes. A triple footbrake system is the result, to which "feel" has been added so that although the travel of the distribution valves is only a few thousandths of an inch, the braking of the car gives exactly the same sensation to the driver as it has done for 40 years . . .'

While not a compact, the Silver Shadow is 6¾ in. shorter and 4¼ in. lower than the Cloud. For the first time the Crewe designers have departed from a separate chassis-frame and body, and adopted a body of monococque construction for the Shadow. The three main reasons for the change are that this type of construction is stronger and stiffer, that the car can be lowered, 5 in. compared with some preceding models, and finally a certain amount of weight can be saved. The majority of the shell is of welded steel construction, but aluminium alloy is used for removable items which do not contribute to the general body stiffness, such as doors, boot lid and bonnet. The backbone of this shell is the underframe which consists basically of the lower half of the car. Built into the underframe assembly are the pick-up points for the front and rear sub-frames and the suspension coil spring housings. The side frames, and the windscreen and rear window frames, complete the main body structure, to which are welded the outer body panels to complete the shell. It will be obvious that every component including the outside skin panels contributes to the strength of the shell. This is not the case, of course, with a separate chassis and body which, for noise-suppression reasons, have to be insulated from one another by rubber mountings, therefore reducing the combined stiffness. Increased stiffness of monocoque construction results in less body flexing arising from general road undulations and cornering forces, and this contributes to better handling and directional stability.

Liberal use of galvanised steel is made in the underframe assembly. This material has a thick coating of zinc, giving it extremely good protection against salt corrosion. It is used for all the underframe box-section members, as well as those parts which are subjected to heavy weathering and stone-blasting effects, especially the areas under the front and rear wings. Further protection is afforded by the phosphatising process, the water-soluble dip stove primer, and the bituminous emulsion underseal.

For the first time on Rolls-Royce, the suspension provides longitudinal and lateral compliance. This is a comparatively new advance in automobile engineering. Road irregularities subject the wheels and suspension to forces in vertical, longitudinal and lateral directions. In the past these forces have been absorbed only by the vertical movements of the wheels, irrespective of these factors' direction, but a method has been devised at Crewe of absorbing the forces *in the direction in which they are applied*. This is achieved by mounting the sub-frames to the body by resilient metal mountings. These comprise stainless-steel springs and wire mesh insulators which have closely-defined spring and damping characteristics. These give the suspension fore and aft flexibility, and to some degree lateral flexibility as well.

Geometry of front and rear suspension is designed so that it compensates for brake dive at the front, and for brake lift at the back, and this is achieved by balancing the extra load on the front springs and the reduction on the rear springs with the braking force at the road. This feature ensures that when braking

at night, the headlamps maintain their adjustment. Another refinement is the elimination of all greasing points on both front and
back suspensions. All joints are now pre-packed and sealed for life.

As outlined earlier by Mr. Grylls, the rear suspension comprises a single trailing arm on each side of the car, and these are
pivoted on rubber bushes attached to the rear-suspension cross-
member. Long coil springs are employed, at the end of which
are the body-height adjusting arms. These springs are insulated
from the body by large rubber isolators minimising the transmission of road and spring noise to the body. The hydraulic
dampers are telescopic, and provide better control of large wheel
movements. The rear suspension cross-member is attached to the
body by the resilient metal mountings already mentioned, and
metal is superior to rubber here, being more compact and also
more stable over longer periods of running. Working in conjunction with these mountings are two radius rods. These are connected to the body and the rear-suspension cross-member by
rubber bushes to reduce transmission noise. A hydraulic telescopic compliance damper is fitted between the body floor and
the rear-suspension cross member:

The independent front suspension is new, and comprises twin
wide-based double triangle levers. The lower triangle is a steel
forging, the upper lever a steel fabrication. These triangle levers
are mounted on the front sub-frame to which are also mounted
the anti-roll bar, the engine, gearbox and steering. The front
sub-frame is also attached to the body by resilient metal mountings, and between the body and the sub-frame there is a transverse locating link. Like the rear suspension, springing at the
front is provided by long coil springs working in conjunction
with telescopic dampers and height-adjusting rams.

Now that a new generation is growing up who never knew a
different Crewe engineering policy, it may be asked why it took
them so long to get around to i.r.s. The official answer is: 'There
can be no doubt that independent four-wheel suspension is a
logical development on all cars. But when applied to Rolls-Royce
and Bentley special problems arose which have taken time and
development to eliminate.'

As to the automatic height control, this system was incorporated
because it maintains the car at a constant height, irrespective of
the load, so the wheel movement remains constant, and softer
springs can be used—with a consequent improvement in comfort.

The levelled height of the car is maintained by four hydraulic rams which act between the upper road spring seats and the body. The car is kept at its designed height and attitude by these rams, which make adjustments whenever the weight or position of the load varies. The rams are controlled by three body-mounted height-control valves mechanically linked to the suspension, and they regulate the flow of hydraulic fluid to and from the rams, to adjust the height and level of the Shadow. There are two height-control valves at the rear and one at the front. Why three valves, and not four? The answer simply is that it would be impossible to reach a state of equilibrium with four.

In addition, a roll-restrictor valve is fitted at the front which ensures that the roll of the car is determined by the characteristics of the road springs and anti-roll bar alone, and is not influenced by the levelling system in any way.

Weight is controlled at two speeds. When driving, the control is sufficiently slow not to react to normal suspension movements, but it will still react to the small, slow changes in weight distribution that may occur. Large changes in weight distribution invariably occur when the car is stationary, as when passengers are entering or leaving. In these circumstances, fast levelling is instigated by opening a door, or by putting the gear-selector into neutral. This energises a solenoid valve allowing the height-control valves to supply high-pressure fluid at a much faster rate to the hydraulic rams.

An integral fluid system for the height control and the disc brakes was chosen, because it is the most simple and reliable way of providing the power. A full servo braking system is essential with a car weighing two tons, and Mr. Grylls has explained some of the reasons why the Royce type of friction servo motor was dropped, due to changed highway conditions.

Brake fluid is used throughout the hydraulic system. It is contained in a large-capacity reservoir mounted under the bonnet, above and to the left side of the engine. This reservoir is divided into separate sections, each feeding one pump, having a sight-glass with the minimum/maximum level clearly marked. The fluid is fed under a slight head to the pumps which are mounted one at either end of the tappet cover on the engine. Each pump is driven by a small integral push-rod and tappet unit operated by eccentrics on the camshaft.

Fluid is pumped into two identical pressure reservoirs mounted

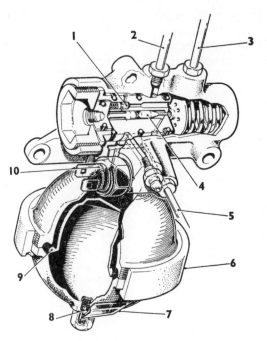

Perspective cut-away diagram of hydraulic accumulator: (1) Inlet valve (2) Low-pressure return valve (3) High-pressure inlet (4) Control valve plunger (5) High-pressure outlet (6) Clamping ring (7) Warning plate (8) Nitrogen charging valve (9) Diaphragm (10) Pressure switch

low down on the left side of the engine. Each accumulator is in the form of a sphere, divided internally by a neoprene diaphragm. Initially the lower half is charged with nitrogen to a pressure of 1,000 lb/sq in., and at this stage the diaphragm is forced against the entire upper surface of the sphere. Fluid is pumped into the accumulator, and the diaphragm gradually takes up a central position as pressure builds up. When pressure reaches 2,500 lb/sq in., a bypass release valve sends excess fluid to the reservoir at zero pressure. Each of the accumulators feeds high-pressure fluid to the various sections of the hydraulic system via control and distribution valves; the front accumulator serves the front caliper of the front brakes, and the lower half of the rear

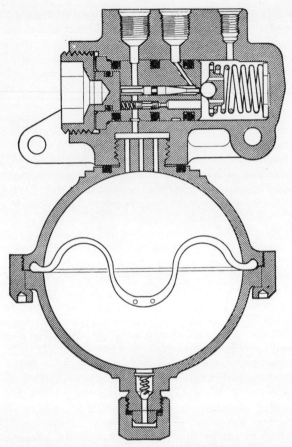

Diagram of accumulator used in the Silver Shadow hydraulic
system. The lower half is charged with nitrogen to a pressure
of 1,000 lb sq. in.

brakes, while the rear accumulator serves the rear caliper of
the front brakes, and the automatic height control.

This triple braking system is complex but, as a member of
the Crewe design team remarked to me: 'The provision of a
braking system which will consistently stop a car weighing
approximately two tons from over 110 mph, without excessive
effort on the part of the driver, without fade after continuous

use, and which will continue to function effectively after a failure of any single mechanical or hydraulic component, is a considerable design problem which called for a much more elaborate arrangement than is common on the majority of cars.'

As we have seen, the self-adjusting brakes are applied by two independent separate high-pressure hydraulic power systems, and one direct, unassisted hydraulic system. All three systems work simultaneously, once the small amount of free travel has been taken up. Of course the handbrake provides a direct and completely separate mechanical brake.

There are two disc-brake calipers to each front wheel, and a dual caliper to each rear wheel. These are applied by two separate power circuits and one direct hydraulic circuit. Each power circuit comprises a separate pressure pump, accumulator, distribution valve, piping and brake-pad cylinders. The circuits are split, the upper half of the rear-wheel calipers being operated by the hydraulic system which comprises a conventional master cylinder operated directly by the brake pedal. This supplies approximately 60 per cent of the rear-wheel braking. This direct hydraulic foot control means that half the rear brakes are effective even when the engine is stopped, and when (rarely) the accumulators are empty. This is to cope with the sort of situation which might arise when a car has been stored for a long time, and requires a tow start.

All the brake pads move a very small distance before the brakes are applied. Their action is virtually instantaneous with the movement of the brake pedal once the small amount of free travel is taken up.

In the interests of stability under heavy emergency braking, Crewe had to ensure that the rear wheels would never lock before the front. This is done in the direct hydraulic system by a 'G-conscious' rear-brake pressure control valve. This regulates the rear-wheel brake pressure in such a way that the rear wheels cannot lock before the front. The action of this valve does not affect the pressure or performance of the rear power brake circuit. The handbrake is of the pull/twist types, as was fitted to the S-series, and operates two wedge-shaped pads on the rear discs. This mechanism incorporates a self-adjusting linkage automatically re-setting the handbrake by means of a ratchet when the brake movement exceeds a pre-determined amount. This overcame a small complaint with some of the older S-series cars that

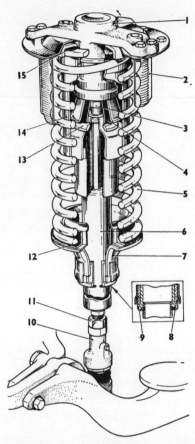

Pictorial view of front spring assembly on the Silver Shadow:
(1) Height control ram (2) Spring pot (3) Damper lock nut
(4) Isolator (5) Road spring (6) Damper (7) Spring seating
(8) Split packing piece (9) Collar (10) Threaded adjuster,
final adjustment for car front height (11) Lock nut (12)
Rubber-canvas seating (13) Distance-piece (14) Road
spring upper housing (15) Rubber-canvas seating
(16) Dustcaps

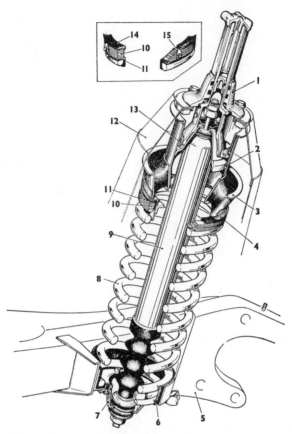

Rear road spring and damper assembly on the Silver Shadow:
(1) Height-control ram (2) Isolator tube and ram piston
seat assembly (3) Spring isolator (4) Road-spring upper
retainer (5) Trailing arm (6) Rubber-canvas seating (7)
Damper lower retaining bracket (8) Road spring (9) Damper
(10) Packing pieces (11) Rubber-canvas seating (10 and 11
comprise the arrangement when six packing pieces or less are
required) (12) Spring pot (13) Locking arrangement,
ram piston to conical seating (14) Rubber-canvas seating,
short type (15) Clip. The inset diagram shows the arrangement
when seven or more packing pieces are required

Above Interior of the Silver Shadow four-door saloon showing Britax automatic safety belts with Autolok reel (standard equipment), steering-column assembly with finger-tip gear-range selector lever. Ammeter and coolant temperature indicator are on facia to the right of the column
Below A rare model, the Silver Cloud III drophead coupé with coachwork by H. J. Mulliner, Park Ward. These convertibles (including the Rolls Bentley S3 series) were discontinued in March, 1966, the Silver Shadow convertible appearing for the first time in September, 1967

Above Silver Cloud III two-door saloon, a unique special model by
H. J. Mulliner, Park Ward. Chassis specification is similar to that of the
standard four-door saloon, but this attractive two-door body is handbuilt
of steel and light alloy. In 1965, at the end of this series, the basic price
was £6,750, £8,158 including UK purchase-tax
Below Silver Shadow convertible, by H. J. Mulliner, Park Ward, an
adaptation of the two-door saloon introduced in 1966. Cooperation
between Pressed Steel and Mulliner, Park Ward made this convertible
possible, despite monocoque saloon construction

the handbrake obstructed the driver's entry into the car when the brakes were becoming worn.

With the introduction of the long-developed Rolls-Royce Girling disc brakes, some drivers expected near-revolutionary results, but Crewe urged restraint. 'As all those who have driven previous models will know, the drum brakes were superb in performance, giving results better than most other cars—including those with discs. Therefore no startling increase in brake performance can be expected.'

However, it is a fact that disc brakes offer greater potential for further development, and, being simplified, give quicker servicing. Even Rolls-Royce were compelled to agree that drum brakes had reached the stage in their development where silence, smoothness and reliability would have been sacrificed to obtain any real increase in brake performance. Now brake pads can be changed in approximately a quarter the time needed to reline a set of drum brakes of comparable performance; no adjustment is needed throughout the life of the pads, as the Rolls-Royce Girling discs are self-adjusting.

Noise suppression was one of the problems in development which took time and ingenuity at Crewe to cure or control. The two common types of noise which discs tend to generate are squeal and squeak. Squeal is caused by the disc itself vibrating at a resonant frequency. If unchecked, this comes out as a loud howl. On the Shadow and T-series this has been successfully damped by wrapping steel wire in a peripheral groove around the disc, and spot-welding a metal strip over it. Squeak, on the other hand, is initiated by pad vibration, and is of shorter duration than squeal. It can be controlled only by careful pad and caliper design. Brake life has been extended by having a large pad area, thus spreading the load. This is achieved by having two brake calipers on each of the front wheels, and a dual caliper on each of the rear wheels. As might be expected, the front pad area is larger than the rear (all discs are 11 in. dia.), since it carries a larger proportion of the braking effort. The problem of pad life is further complicated on all cars by a phenomenon known as wet-weather wear. It is known that the inboard pads can wear out more quickly in wet weather due to water-borne grit adhering to the discs, giving them an abrasive surface. This has been virtually eliminated on the Silver Shadow by positioning the disc close to the wheel, while the caliper assemblies shield

I

most of the disc from the direct flow of airborne water. Cooling holes are drilled at the base of the discs.

As we have seen, the automatic gearbox was introduced at Crewe in 1953. The box as used in the Silver Shadow has been redesigned to incorporate several new features, and of course now there is electric control.

The critical sequence for the gearbox has always been the third-to-second and second-to-third gear change, entailing the simultaneous operation of two clutches and two brake bands. To enable smoother gear-changes to be made, a free-wheel mechanism is incorporated, this taking the place of the rear brake band in first and second gear. This mechanism free-wheels on the over-run in first and second gears, and results in particularly smooth third-to-second down-shifts.

In certain countries it is a legal requirement that full engine braking is available, and this is provided only when range 2 is selected.

Aluminium is now used for the gearbox main casing, and many of the internal parts. Its lighter weight counteracts the additional weight of the free-wheel mechanism, and its better heat-dissipating properties, coupled with the ventilated bell-housing, reduce the possibility of overheating. In the past, continuous heavy traffic operation tended to overheat the box, to the detriment of the brake and clutch linings. An under-bonnet dipstick and filler tube are now provided, as a very low fluid level in any automatic box can have disastrous results. It is now much easier to check level and top up.

The gear-selection lever on the steering column is in effect a five-position switch connected to an electrical actuator on the side of the box. As a precaution against the unlikely failure of any part of the circuit, or if a component becomes overloaded, a thermal cut-out breaks the circuit. This is situated in the fuse-box under the facia panel, and is re-set by pushing a red button. There is an additional safeguard which gave the technical Press some mild amusement when the Silver Shadow was first driven. The device is a 'get-you-home' gear selector lever on the left side of the gearbox, and can be operated manually through the transmission tunnel, with the aid of the wheel-disc tommy-bar in the tool-kit. Access to this side of the gearbox is through a hole in the floor after lifting the carpet.

In normal driving, the electric gearchange lever allows the

driver to override the box, and, if he wishes, to anticipate a necessary gear-change. Sitting at the wheel, it will be noticed there are positions for reverse, neutral and three forward ranges, marked R, N, 4, 3 and 2. In position 4, the box changes up and down through all four forward gears automatically, and this is used for all normal driving irrespective of speed. In position 3, the box will not change from third to fourth unless the car is travelling at over 74 mph, when a safety change into fourth gear prevents the engine from over-revving. This range is used where it is felt that third-gear engine braking or acceleration is required. The speed at which the 3–4 change occurs is slightly higher than in 4 range, giving the car a better full-throttle performance, so it is a useful range for fast driving in traffic.

In position 2, the gearbox is locked in second gear, and can be changed only by moving the lever. It is used mainly for engine braking on steep descents, for ceremonial processions or in heavy traffic where it is obviously advantageous to lock the gearbox in a low gear. In position R, reverse gear is engaged when the engine is running, but if the engine is stopped then the transmission is locked and can be used as a parking brake. A safety feature incorporated in the Shadow transmission for the first time ensures that when the ignition is switched off, the transmission may be locked by engaging reverse, but cannot be disengaged until the ignition is switched on. This is an important safety feature, in circumstances where children play with the gearchange lever when the car is left on a steep hill.

To the newcomer to automatic transmission, all the foregoing may sound complex, but it will be appreciated there is no clutch pedal, no gear synchromesh changes to bother with, and moving the gearchange lever will not result in damage to the box at any time; if the car's speed is not appropriate to the gear, *then nothing happens*. For example, third gear will engage only under 70 mph, second gear under 40 mph, and reverse under 8 mph. The parking brake will operate only with the lever in reverse, and the engine stopped. At night the numbered positions on the quadrant are illuminated when the sidelamp circuit is on.

Development of the V8 power unit has been dealt with in preceding chapters, but there are a number of differences between the Silver Shadow engine and that in the Silver Cloud III. Cylinder heads have been redesigned to give better flow, and spark plugs are positioned in the top of the head, so are more accessible from the bonnet. A better air silencer and cleaner unit is now situated under the front wing, which enables its size to be increased. High-pressure hydraulic pumps are situated at both ends of the tappet cover, and supply high-pressure fluid to the two accumulators also mounted on the engine. The cooling system incorporates a separate header tank, so ensuring that air and coolant are not mixed and circulated together. Detail alterations have been made to carburetters, the exhaust manifold, sump, dipstick layout, and the front gear casing. In the six years prior to the complete establishment of the Silver Shadow, the engine has of course undergone continuous improvement, with detail changes to carburetters, heads, pistons, connecting-rods, camshaft, crankshaft, tappets and distributor.

By 1968 the outline specification is as follows. The unit is an over-square 90-deg.V, having a capacity of 6,230 cc. Crankcase and cylinders are cast as one piece from an aluminium alloy having a high silicon content. Pistons run in cast-iron wet liners giving better cooling and reduced bore distortion. During initial assembly, each piston is matched to its appropriate liner to make sure the required running tolerances are obtained. The aluminium cylinder heads are fitted with austenitic iron seats, cast iron inlet valve guides, and phosphor-bronze exhaust guides.

The crankshaft is forged from chrome molybdenum steel, nitride hardened; and as described previously in Chapter Three, every crankshaft is forged with a small test-piece included which, when received at Crewe, is tested mechanically and chemically in the laboratory. The shaft runs in five shell bearings, and an interesting feature here is that all the main-bearing and big-end bolts are ground to a waisted form so that the strain imposed when they are tightened is distributed uniformly along the bolt. The camshaft is of cast iron, and driven from the crankshaft through helical gears; the gear on the crankshaft is of steel, while that on the camshaft is of aluminium. Apart from the obvious fact that the expansion of aluminium under normal operating conditions largely counteracts increased backlash (which would otherwise be caused by expansion of the crankcase), the alloy gear has a lower inertia, resulting in reduced stresses and subsequent wear in the gear teeth caused by torsional vibration of the crankshaft. The valves are of high-grade steel, and the seats and stem tips of the exhaust valves are coated with a cobalt-nickel alloy which is particularly durable in high temperature. Similarly, the crown face of each exhaust valve is treated with a nickel-chrome alloy to prevent preignition during high-speed running for prolonged periods.

Engine oil is circulated by a gear-type pump mounted on the front of the crankcase and driven by the crankshaft through skew gears. Oil is drawn from the sump through a fine mesh gauze strainer and delivered from the pump through a full-flow filter to the bearings, uniform pressure delivery being maintained by a relief valve in the sump. Oil is fed under high pressure to the main and big-end bearings of the crankshaft, the camshaft, hydraulic tappets and the timing gears; from the tappets oil is fed through hollow push-rods to lubricate the hemi-spherical seat in the rocker arm into which the push-rod fits. Hollow push-rods provide maximum strength with the minimum weight; lubricant is fed under reduced pressure to the o.h. valve gear through hollow studs. Gudgeon-pins and cylinder walls are, of course, splash-lubricated from the crankcase.

Vintage Rolls-Royce owners may mourn the passing of the now-classic twin-jet automatic expanding Royce carburetter used prior to the introduction of the Stromberg type, and old-time Bentley owners will regret the days are no more when 'slopers' were fitted, and 'SU's looked like SU's.' The fact remains that the special SU-type carburetters (twin HD8's, modified) now fitted to the Silver Shadow and T-series have several special features not to be found in the standard SU. Each carburetter feeds four cylinders, two in each bank. In the R.-R. pattern, the float-chamber is modified to insulate fuel from engine heat, and so to minimise evaporation. Furthermore, throttle spindles are of stainless steel. It was found that brass spindles are naturally more subject to wear, which results in air-leaks and weak mixture. There are other detail differences, and even vintage lovers like the way the cars are now turned out, with the SU's highly polished to match the rest of the engine, and all visible screws and levers cadmium-plated.

A Crewe-designed automatic choke mechanism assists cold starting without risk of engine damage by excessively rich mixture. As with Silver-Wraith-type techniques, before starting the Shadow engine the throttle pedal is fully depressed and released. This sets the fast-idle cam on the carburetter controls in relation to engine temperature, and gives a higher engine tick-over speed than is normally used for idling. The basic operation of the choke mechanism is controlled by a temperature-sensitive bi-metal coil over which air, heated by the exhaust gas, is passed. Immediately the engine fires this air begins to warm up, and the bi-metal coil starts opening the choke. If the under-bonnet temperature is below 15-deg. C, immediately the ignition is switched on an electrically-operated solenoid holds the choke closed for a short time, this being controlled by a thermal delay switch. Above this degree of chill, a temperature-sensitive switch breaks the circuit to the solenoid.

The generator, coolant pump, power-assisted-steering pump and (when fitted) the refrigeration compressor, are driven from the crankshaft pulley through pre-stretched belts which are in matched pairs. An interesting design detail is to be found in the fan, the blades being set at irregular intervals to reduce fan noise.

On the facia is a comprehensive set of warning systems which can alert the driver and enable him to stop the car before damage is done. There is the usual red ignition warning lamp, and an oil-pressure warning lamp as well as a pressure gauge. In a composite warning-lamp panel there is an array of lamps. Two red lamps give individual warning when the pressure in either of the hydraulic accumulators falls below the safe level. They may light up when the car has been standing idle for a long time, but should be extinguished immediately the engine has started. Ever since the days of the '25' in the 1930's a green fuel-level warning lamp has been provided on the instrument panel to show when only a few gallons are left in the tank. Today the circuit comes on when the level of the 24-gallon tank falls to three gallons, and a new feature for the Shadow is a series resistance to dim this green pilot when the sidelamps are on; this reduces the glare of the low-fuel lamp at night. A coolant-level yellow warning lamp shows if the level of the coolant falls below the safe limit (as the system is pressurised, this avoids some delay in checking the level), and just beside the warning-lamp panel there is a small button which, in addition to registering the engine oil level on the fuel gauge (a neat idea which came in in 1947, with the Silver Wraith), now also illuminates all four warning lamps in this panel. This enables a driver to test, say once a day, for possible bulb failure. There is the customary main beam warning light contained in the speedometer dial, and trafficator bulbs similarly arranged, flashing when either left or right indicator is switched. A double-purpose pilot is that for the handbrake; the little warning light is illuminated once the ignition is switched on, and until the handbrake is released. And once it is released, this pilot is then switched so that it becomes a warning lamp telling the driver if either of the rear tail stop lamps fail. Finally, above the top of the screen, positioned between the sun visors, is the switch for the hazard warning system, which also incorporates a pilot lamp. This hazard switch causes all four indicators, two front, two rear, to flash automatically; this has always been a welcome system in many countries, and in recent years has been legalised in the United Kingdom. At night it prevents a Silver Shadow being accidentally rammed by an oncoming car if for any reason the Shadow's driver cannot pull completely off the road.

While the nursery-rhyme lyric writer says that little girls are made of sugar and spice and all things nice, Silver Shadows nowadays are made of nice things far more complex, such as polytetrafluroethylene and—of course—aluminium. In fact about 350 lb (160 kg) of aluminium is used in each Shadow.

The difference in strength between aluminium and cast iron is surprisingly small, and the weight of the alloy is about half that of iron. However Crewe have conducted extensive research to overcome the problems of using 'ali' in cars; its disadvantages include the fact that it is difficult to weld, and that pressing panels from sheet aluminium is not an easy process. Today Rolls-Royce use more aluminium per car than any other United Kingdom manufacturer. Body aluminium castings include fuel filter body, fuel-pump body, horn trumpets and various parts of the hydraulic system. The transmission includes such aluminium castings as those for the casing, rear servo accumulator, fluid coupling bell housing, gearcase covers, differential housing, and the automatic gearbox 'brain box,' which is a pressure die casting instead of the more common sand-casting. In the engine apart from the integrally-cast crankcase and block, aluminium is used for the heads, rocker covers, camshaft timing-gear covers, distributor housing, pistons, induction manifold, oil pump body, water-pump housing and many smaller components.

Those who look mildly surprised at the complexity and extent of some of these light alloy castings will be told by Crewe engineers: 'Well, we used to have the crankcase, gearbox and steering-box in cast aluminium. That was in 1906 . . .'

Stainless steel is used extensively because it is more durable than chromium plating, and a special alloy highly resistant to chemical and atmospheric attack is used for window frames, running-board tread plates, sill mouldings, the centre bonnet moulding, wheel discs, the exhaust silencers, and the resilient metal mountings for sub-frames and exhaust systems—and of course also for the radiator shell and mascot.

Shades of the early Spirit of Ecstasy . . . the girl on the Silver Shadow is now collapsible. This is because rigidly-mounted mascots are considered dangerous in certain countries. It is now possible to remove the normal rigid mascot by means of an Allen key in the tool-kit, and to substitute a button instead of the mascot whilst travelling in a country where rigid mascots are illegal. The collapsible Spirit is fitted to cars exported to such countries, or is an optional extra elsewhere. As all Rolls-Royce mascots have a high 'scrounge-rate,' this matter of providing a detachable figure might have introduced some risk; however, it is still impossible for a thief to remove the mascot unless he has access under the bonnet. Incidentally, there is no collapsible Bentley mascot, since its base is too long and too narrow to enable it to collapse safely in all directions, in the event of an impact.

There has always been a rather special magic about Rolls-Royce chassis numbers and letters, and in such circles as the Twenty-Ghost Club members never indicate their registration (Road Fund) number, but only the car's chassis number. So far as the Silver Shadow and T-series are concerned, the letters indicate a pleasant sense of humour on the part of the Crewe engineering team. Despite the emphasis on the Bentley T, at Crewe the whole series is definitely Shadow. Thus the routine United Kingdom series is SRH, which stands for 'Shadow right-hand drive,' and the Bentley version has the chassis series starting at SBH, 'Shadow Bentley Home' (right-hand-drive). SRX is 'Shadow Rolls Export, while the remaining versions are CRH (coachbuilt Rolls, Home), CRX (coachbuilt Rolls, Export), and equivalent CBH and CBX (coachbuilt Bentley, Home/Export).

The first to come off the production line was a Bentley, not a Rolls-Royce. It bears the serial SBH 1001. So, as these things nowadays have collectors' value, the owner of SRH 1002 (presumably the first Silver Shadow) has a car worth considerably more than he may realise.

SILVER SHADOW SPECIFICATION

ENGINE

Bore	4·1 in.
Stroke	3·6 in.
No. of cylinders	8, in two banks of 4
Capacity	6,230 cc (380·5 cu. in.)
Compression ratio	9:1 (8:1 optional)
Firing order	Taking A as the right-hand bank viewed from the driver's seat: A1, B1, A4, B4, B2, A3, B3, A2
Spark plugs	Champion N 16 Y
Spark plug gap	0·023–0·028 in.
Distributor	Vacuum and centrifugal mechanical automatic advance/retard
Distributor contacts	0·014–0·016 in.
Ignition timing	2° before TDC
Vibration damper	Metalastic bonded rubber
Valve-gear	Overhead in-line, push-rod operated, hydraulic self-adjusting tappets
Oil filtration	Full-flow, paper element filter
Fuel pumps	Twin SU, electric, independent
Carburetters	Twin SU HD8 side-draught diaphragm, with automatic choke
Air-silencer	Acoustic silencer and cleaner, under-wing mounted, with paper or oil wetted wire-mesh filter element
Coolant	Pressurised at 7 lb/sq. in. Separate header tank, centrifugal pump and wax-filled thermostat

GEARBOX

Rolls-Royce manufacture. Four forward gears and reverse, with over-riding hand and kick-down change control. Electric gear selection by steering-column lever.

Ratios	Gearbox ratio	Overall ratio
1st	3·28	11·75
2nd	2·63	8·10
3rd	1·45	4·46
4th	1·0	3·08
Reverse	4·3	13·25
Top-gear mph	26·2 mph at 1,000 rpm	

FINAL DRIVE

Hypoid bevel gears in aluminium final drive casing mounted to cross-member which is attached to body resilient metal mountings. Single-piece large-diameter propeller shaft with one ball-and-trunnion constant-velocity universal joint, and one needle-roller Hooke universal joint.

HYDRAULIC SYSTEM

Reservoir	Under bonnet, with two sight glass level indicators
Pumps	Two camshaft-driven piston pumps
Accumulators	Two under bonnet, maintained at 2,500 lb/sq. in. to operate power brakes and automatic height control

BRAKES

System	Disc to all wheels, two single calipers to each front disc, one caliper to each rear disc.
Safety features	Three independent footbrake systems, plus handbrake. Brake pressure control valve for rear wheels.
Handbrake	Mechanical, with equaliser link to operate on rear discs

SILVER SHADOW SPECIFICATION

SUSPENSION

System — Full independent to all wheels

Front — Double triangle lever coil-spring suspension, telescopic hydraulic shock dampers, automatic height control, brake dive compensation

Rear — Coil-spring suspension by single trailing arm. Telescopic hydraulic shock dampers, brake lift compensation. Automatic height control

STEERING

System — Re-circulating ball, power-assisted through rotary-valve torsion-bar-operated control valve

Overall steering ratio — 19·32

Turns (lock/lock) — 4

Turning circle — 38 ft

ELECTRICAL SYSTEM

Generator — 12v with current/voltage compensated control. Max output 35a,13.5v

System — Negative earth

Alternator (as fitted to cars with refrigeration) — 12v, with transistorised voltage regulator. Max output 45a, 13.5v

Battery — Dagenite Easyfil, 11-plate 68 a.h. at 20-hour rating. Fitted on left side of luggage compartment

TYRES

Size — 8·45 × 15 low-profile

Pressures (cold)

Front — 24 lb/sq in. (1·69 kg/sq. cm)

Rear — 24 lb/sq. in. (1·69 kg/sq. cm)

Front/rear for continuous high-speed running — 28 lb/sq. in. (1·97 kg/sq. cm)

LUBRICATION

(Greasing required only at steering and height-control ball-joints every 12,000 miles—20,000 km. All other joints sealed for life)

Capacities	*Imp*	*US*	*Metric (litres)*
Fuel tank	23½ gals	28 gals	107
Coolant	28 pints	33½ pints	16
Sump	14½ pints	17½ pints	7·6
Gearbox (RHD)	24 pints	29 pints	13·6
(LHD)	18⅔ pints	22½ pints	10·6
Final drive unit	4½ pints	5 pints	2·5
Steering-pump reservoir	3 pints	3½ pints	1·7
Hydraulic system	4 pints	4½ pints	2·3

INDEX

Accumulators, hydraulic, and nitrogen pressure reservoirs, self-levelling system, 124 et seq.

Air silencer, for Silver Shadow, 137

Alloy castings, used by Rolls-Royce Ltd. in 1906, 130

Alpes Maritimes, test of Silver Cloud III in, 77

Alternators, fitted to Silver Shadow cars with refrigeration facilities, 139

Assets, trading of Rolls-Royce Ltd., 12, 24

Austenal foundry, at Crewe, 47

Autocar and *The Autocar*, 6, 15, 65, 117

Automatic choke operation, 133

Avery dynamic balancing technique, Crewe, 43

Bailey, S. B., MSc, 93, 97

Ball, Kenneth, and use of historic Rolls-Royce documentary material, 6

Barker, Ronald, visit to Crewe, 42

Barnoldswick, Rolls-Royce plant at, and high-voltage electron beam welding technique, 51

Beaulieu, Lord Montagu of, 47

Beaverbrook, Lord, and Baron Hives, wartime discussions on Rolls-Royce tank and aero-engine production, 34

Benson, Elizabeth, and report on test of the Silver Shadow, 6, 117

Bentley and Bentley Motors, 21, 68, 74

Birfield, transmission components, 42

Book of the Phantoms and early Company History, 18, 66

Borg Warner Type 8 automatic transmission, as used on Vanden Plas Princess R, 93

Boyd, Maxwell, 6, 116, 117

B-range, industrial Rolls-Royce engines, 81

Brinell, hardness factors, 85

Bristol Siddeley and Rolls-Royce Ltd., 23, 25

Brooks, Tony, 6, 98 et seq.

Cathcart, Helen, and use of Rolls-Royce cars by HRH the Duke of Edinburgh, 6, 110

Chassis series, Silver Shadow and Bentley T, 136

Chromium-plating of cylinder bores, 69

Claremont, Ernest, partner in the early venture of Rolls and Royce, 29

Component testing, Crewe, 43

Computer facilities, aiding aero engine and the Rolls-Royce Motorcar Division, 59

Connecting-rod design, 44

Coolant flow, V8 engines, 86

Coyle, J. C., and vibration testing, Crewe, 52

Crankshaft testing, 44, 88, 132

Crewe works, 33, 37 et seq.